John A. Porter

New Standard Guide of the City of Washington and Environs

Volume 1

John A. Porter

New Standard Guide of the City of Washington and Environs
Volume 1

ISBN/EAN: 9783337182441

Printed in Europe, USA, Canada, Australia, Japan

Cover: Foto ©Andreas Hilbeck / pixelio.de

More available books at **www.hansebooks.com**

NEW

STANDARD GUIDE

OF THE CITY OF

Washington and Environs

WITH

MAP AND INDICATOR

FOR LOCATING

ALL POINTS OF INTEREST

AND

THE PRINCIPAL BUSINESS HOUSES.

WASHINGTON, D. C.:
ARLINGTON PUBLISHING CO.
CORCORAN BUILDING.
1886.

Printed by
JUDD & DETWEILER,
Washington, D. C.

PREFACE.

In offering their new Guide to the public, the publishers desire to call especial attention to the following features:

(1.) The Descriptions of all Points of Interest in the City and Vicinity are presented in terse, clear, and accurate form; they are arranged alphabetically and fully indexed, so as to afford easy reference.

(2.) The Appendices contain Full Lists and Interesting Statistics concerning the National and Municipal Governments, and the Various Local Organizations—Religious, Charitable, Educational, Mercantile, Social, etc.

(3.) The Select classified Lists of Trades and Professions together with the Business Cards, at the end of the book, represent the Principal Firms of the city. Introduced in a novel and attractive manner, this Department will be found to be one of the most useful and interesting in the book.

(4.) The Colored Map which accompanies the Guide contains an ingenious Tape Attachment by which even a stranger can locate, instantly, all points of interest and the leading business houses mentioned in the Guide. This is by far the best patent map ever produced, and, to every resident of Washington, is alone worth many times the price of the Guide.

As may be seen from inspection, the Guide and Map serve as a Pocket Directory, which will prove as indispensable to visitors and in the homes of citizens as the Large Directory is to Merchants.

Having spared neither time nor expense to make their publication worthy of the title which it bears—"Standard Guide," of the National Capital—the publishers are justified in believing that the work will be cordially received and merit a wide sale at the hands of the public.

TABLE OF CONTENTS.

LIST OF ILLUSTRATIONS.

INSTRUCTIONS

For finding on Map any place mentioned in the Guide.

Places in this guide are alphabetically arranged with figures attached, one in the column for margin, the other in the column for tape. To find, for instance, the location of Lincoln Park, margin 51, tape 30, place the tape on the corresponding marginal number on the map, and read the other number corresponding on the tape, and Lincoln Park will be found on the map and under the number of the tape. Or to find Water street, 19–56, as before, place the tape on the marginal number designated, and under the corresponding number on the tape is the name of the street printed on the map, the location of which is desired.

The tape is divided into numbered sections, each of which scales 880 feet; also divided into miles and fractions thereof.

To find the distance from one point to another place the tape conveniently at either point, and lay it along the route desired to be measured, turn it in corners if necessary, and when the other point is reached read off the number of sections and compute them, 5,280 feet to the mile, or read off the corresponding mile measure. For instance, the distance is wanted from the Schuetzen Park, 20–36, to the President's Mansion, 46–46, along Seventh street and Pennsylvania avenue, place the divided end of the tape on Seventh street on the map and at the Schuetzen Park until it reaches the corner of Pennsylvania avenue, there turn it and run it along said avenue until you get to the President's Mansion, there read off the number of sections, and the distance is thus in either case found to be four miles.

The city is divided in four quarters—east and west by the line of North and South Capitol streets extended, and north and south by the line of East Capitol street extended, these lines crossing in the center of the Capitol building, which is plainly illustrated by the coloring of the map, and hence the appellation of northwest, southeast, &c., to streets, thereby designating the particular quarter in which the street is located.

All streets running north and south are called by numbers; east or west from North and South Capitol streets.

All streets running east and west are called by letters of the alphabet in similar manner counted from the line of the East Capitol street extended.

The decimal system of house numbering is used, allowing one hundred numbers for each square.

Avenues named after States in the Union run diagonally from different centers, generally converging towards the Capitol Building or the President's Mansion.

DIRECTORY OF AVENUES AND STREETS.

☞ For plan of streets, system of numbering, abbreviations, etc., see preceding page.

	N.	Y.
Alexander row, fr 1136 N H av	23	50
Armory st sw, fr 311 4½	55	29
Bates st nw, fr 1512 N Cap	22	45
Bellevue ter nw, fr 2611 N	27	48
Berry row nw, fr R ab 21st	23	50
Boundary st ne, fr N Cap ab P	40	36
Boundary st nw, fr N Cap ab P	29	42
Brainard st nw, fr 1728 P	22	46
California st se, fr 1st to 2d	48	38
Canal st se, from S Cap and G	57	33
Canal st sw, fr 2d and B	58	36
Caroline st nw, fr 1919 15th	24	43
Caroline ter nw	40	44
Carroll pl se, fr 12 1st	54	35
Carroll st se, fr 214 1st	54	35
Central av ne, fr Lincoln av	32	34
Chicago st ne, fr 1st to 2d ab F	46	35
Colfax st ne, fr 3, to M ab 1st	41	35
Colfax st nw, fr 5th ab Sumner	28	38
College-hill ter	30	38
Columbia av nw, fr 13th and Boundary	21	42
Columbia st nw, fr 927 O	32	41
Connecticut av, fr H and Lexington pl	31	47
Cooke pl nw, from 3001 Q	16	52
Corcoran st nw, fr 1902 18th	28	44
Cottage pl nw, fr 1209 T	22	45
Covington st nw, fr 927 Q	31	41
Crandall row, see Marion st nw	33	40
Crescent st nw, fr Columbia av	17	42
Dartmouth st, fr Sherman av	18	42
Deer row nw, fr 2149 P	17	52
Decatur st, fr N Cap bet O and P	32	35
Defrees st nw, fr 806 N Cap	44	36
Delaware av ne, fr the Capitol	45	35
Delaware av sw, fr the Capitol	60	37
De Sales st nw, fr 1126 17th	34	47
Duddington pl se, 1st to C	56	35
Dudley pl nw, fr 171 2d	50	34
Dumbarton av nw, fr Rock crk	14	54
East st nw, fr 27th ab P	20	53
East Capitol st, fr the Capitol	52	33
Ellis st Cottage Hill, fr Park	13	43
Elm st, fr LeDroit av to Larch	28	38
Evans av, fr Sheridan av Hillsdale	64	26
Emery row nw, bet 25th and 26th ab H	40	52
Erie st nw, fr Columbia av	16	42
Executive pl, Pa av fr 15th	42	46
Farragut st nw, fr 7th-st rd	19	36
Fayette st Gtn, now 35th st nw	11	55
Fifteenth-and-a-half st nw	42	46
Franklin pl, fr 803 to 921 13th	41	44
Franklin sq nw, 13th bt I and K	41	44
Franklin st, fr N J av to 6th ab P	34	39
French st nw, fr 1208 9th	28	41
Gay st Gtn, now N st nw	38	54
Georgia av se, fr S Cap and Q	57	29
Georgia av sw, fr S Cap and Q	67	34
Gilman st nw, see Maple av nw	29	39
Grace st nw, fr 1616 32d	25	54
Grant av, fr Boundary and 10th	22	39
Grant pl nw, fr 720 9th	40	42
Grant st, fr Pine to Brown rd	18	42
Greene st Gtn, now 29th st nw	25	53
Half st sw, fr 3d P	64	45
Hamilton pl nw, fr 1441 K	39	44
Harewood av nw, fr Boundary and 4th	30	34
Henrich st nw, fr 1906 M	29	44
High st Gtn, now 32d st nw	29	53
Hillyer av nw, fr 1632 20th	23	46
Hope av ne, fr D to E ab 12th	47	30
Hopkins st nw, fr O ab 20th	26	48
Howard Univ'y Grds, 7th st rd	24	37
Huron st nw, fr Columbia av	19	42
Indiana av nw, fr 1st and C	49	38
Ingle pl se, on C bet 1st and 2d	55	35
Iowa circle nw, 13th and P	31	43
Irvin st nw, fr 7th st rd	19	37
Jackson pl, see Lexington pl	42	46
Jackson st ne, fr 211 N Cap	44	36
Jefferson pl nw, fr 1218 Conn av	30	48
Johnson av nw, fr 1417 R	27	43
Keating av, fr Lincoln av	28	30
Kendall Green, Boundary bet 7th and 9th ne	45	33
Kenesaw st nw, fr Sherman av	17	39
Kentucky av, fr 12th and E Cap	54	29
Kenyon st nw, fr Sherman av	18	39
Kingman pl nw, fr 1517 P	31	43
Knowlton r'w sw, bt ½ M and N	62	36
Lafayette sq, see Madison pl nw	41	46
Langdon ter nw, on 6th st ext	26	38
Lanier pl ne, bt C A	56	33
Larch st, fr Boundary and 6th	26	38
Laurel av nw, fr Brown ab Oak	16	39
Lawrence st nw, fr 14th ab R	22	44
LeDroit pk, village nth side of Boundary bet 2d and 7th nw	29	37
Lexington pl nw, fr Pa av bet 16th and 17th	42	46
Lexington ter nw, fr 1515 Q	31	43
Lindsey row, see Alexander row	23	50
Liberty st nw, fr 1301 W	21	41
Liberty st sw, fr 411 3d	62	41
Lincoln sq E Cap, fr 11th	51	30
Lincoln st ne, fr 7th st rd	21	38
Linden st nw, fr Boundary and N J av	30	38
Louisiana av, from 4½ and D	50	41
McClelland st nw	28	38
McPherson sq nw, 15th fr I	41	45
Madison av nw, fr 1622 18th	25	45

	M.	T.
Madison pl, fr Pa av bet 15th and 16th	42	46
Madison st Gtn, now V st nw	8	52
Madison st nw, fr 621 M	37	40
Magnolia av, fr Brightwood	17	35
Maine av sw, fr 101 3d to 100 6th	55	30
Mable av nw, fr Le Droit av	30	38
Marion st nw, fr 621 P	32	40
Market sp Gtn, now Potomac av	16	58
Market sp Pa av fr 7th to 9th	50	41
Market st Gtn, now 33d st nw	13	54
Maryland av ne, fr the Capitol	47	32
Maryland av sw, fr the Capitol	56	40
Massachusetts av se, fr N Cap to 12th	50	31
Massachusetts av nw, fr N Cap to 23d	30	45
Massachusetts av se, fr 12th to 19th	52	27
Meridan av Mer hill, fr Boundary	20	42
Meridan av Mt P fr Brown	16	40
Meridian hill, fr Boundary	19	43
Mossmore av nw, fr Erie	18	43
Mill st Gtn, now 27th st nw	23	52
Missouri av nw, fr 100 3d	52	39
Monroe st Gtn, now 27th st nw	23	52
Montgomery st Gtn, now 28th st	19	52
Morris st nw, fr Columbia av to Meridian av Mer hill	19	43
Morrison st nw, fr 7th st rd	18	36
Mt Pleasant, a village on Piney-branch rd 1 mile from city	15	38
Mt Pleasant av, fr Park Mt P	15	39
Mt Pleasant st nw, fr 7th-st rd	15	39
Mt Vernon pl, K bet 7th and 9th	41	41
Murdoch row nw, fr 1800 20th	31	42
Myrtle st ne, fr N Cap to 1st ab I	43	36
New Hampshire av nw, fr 27th and E	33	49
New Jersey av nw, fr the Capitol to Boundary	42	38
New Jersey av se, from the Capitol to 2d and N	56	35
New York av ne, fr N Cap and N	39	37
New York av nw, fr N Cap and N	43	44
Nichols pl ne, from 34 B	50	36
North av, fr Lincoln av	29	33
North st Gtn, now 26th st nw	22	51
North Capitol st, from the Capitol to Boundary	43	36
North Carolina ave ne, from 12th and E Capitol	49	28
North Carolina av se, from N J av and E	56	34
Oak st nw, fr Centre to Brown	15	42
Oakland av nw, fr Columbia rd	17	43
Ohio av sw, fr 12th and B	59	44
Olive av nw, fr Rock creek	24	52
Ontario av, fr Bound'y and 17th	16	43
Oregon av nw, fr N H av ab S	22	45
Park pl ne, from 11th ab B	49	30
Park row sw, from 311 13½	58	43
Park st, fr Lincoln	25	37
Parker row sw, fr L bt 1st and 2d	61	36
Pennsylvania ave nw, fr the Capitol to 29th and M	48	43
Pennsylvania ave se, from the Capitol to Anacostia river	54	33
Peters st nw, see Centre st nw	15	39
Philadelphia pl nw, fr 1011	42	42
Philadelphia row se, 11th nr A	52	30
Pierce st nw, from 1140 N Cap	40	37
Pine st, fr Columbia rd to Park	17	41
Pleasant st, fr Lincoln	24	38
Pleasant st Mt P, fr Park	15	39
Pomeroy av Hillsdale, fr Sheridan av	65	23
Pomeroy st nw, fr Le Droit av	28	38
Poplar st nw, fr 1414 27th	19	52
Potomac av nw, fr 3250 Water	17	55
Presbyterian al nw, fr 1417 I	40	45
President sq, see Executive pl	47	46
Princeton st nw, fr 11th ext to Piney-branch rd	22	40
Prospect av nw, fr 1230 32d	24	53
Prospect av Wash'n hts	18	47
Prospect st ne, from Lincoln av	32	34
Prospect st nw, fr Columbia av	18	43
Rawling sq nw, N Y av fr 18th	47	48
R. I. av nw, fr Boundary nr 4th	32	44
Richardson pl nw, fr 1705 N J av	31	38
Ridge st nw, fr 1220 4th	37	39
Riggs st nw, fr 13th to 14th ab R	28	43
Riggs-market al nw, fr 1436 P	29	44
Read st Gtn, now U st nw	10	52
Roanoke st nw, fr 11th ext	21	39
Rock st Gtn, now 27th st nw	23	52
Ruppert st nw, fr 2222 12th	25	41
Samson st, see Madison av nw	28	45
School st nw, fr Kenesaw av to Park	19	39
School st sw, fr 4½ bet Va av	59	39
Scott pl nw, 16th and N	32	46
Sheridan st nw, fr 7th-st rd	20	37
Sherman av, fr Bound'y and 9th	25	39
Sherman row ne, fr 100 F	46	35
Sherman st nw, fr 18th ab Q	24	47
Six-and-a-half st sw, fr 620 D	59	40
Sixteenth-and-a-half st nw	42	46
Soldiers' Home rd	23	33
South av, fr Lincoln av	28	32
South st nw, fr 1000 31st to 32d	24	54
South Capitol st, fr the Capitol	61	35
South Carolina av se, fr 2d and G	54	30
Spruce st nw, fr Le Droit av	28	37
Stanton av, fr Nichols av	66	27
Stanton pl ne, C fr 4th to 6th	49	33
Steuben st nw, fr 7th-st rd	19	37
Stoddart st Gtn, now Q st nw	13	53
Stoughton st nw, from Piney-branch rd	18	40
Summit ter ne, from 212 2d	49	34
Sumner av, fr Nichols av	65	27
Sumner st nw, from 5th ext	22	37
Sunderland pl nw, fr 1314 20th	27	48
Superior av nw, fr Meridian av	19	43
Talbert av, fr Nichols av to Stanton av	65	27
Tennessee av, fr 12th and E Cap	47	28
Terrace at Cottage Hill, fr Park	15	39
Trumbull st nw, fr 7th-st rd	21	37
Tudor pl nw, fr 1518 31st	16	53
Turner st nw, see Columbia st	33	41

	M.	T.
Union st sw, fr 430 M to st	46	39
University hill, see Howard University	24	33
Valley st nw, fr [illegible]	18	33
Vermont av fr Madison pl and H	35	44
Virginia av nw, fr 17th and B	46	53
Virginia av se, fr S Cap and E	59	33
Virginia av sw, fr S Cap and E	52	34
Wallach st nw, fr 7th st rd	19	37
Warner st nw, fr 1600 N J av	34	38
Warren st Gtn, now 37th st **nw**	7	34
Washington heights, at 3d grd	18	47
Washington st Gtn, now 30th st	22	53
Washington st nw, fr 722 4th	44	39
Washington ter ne, fr 12 3d	50	34
Water st nw, fr 21st and Rec 26th and fr 29th and K to 37th	18	36
Water st sw, fr P nr 4½	65	45
West st Gtn, now P st nw	17	52
West Market sp nw, K fr 26th	35	49
Whitney av nw, fr 7th st rd to soldiers' home	14	35
Willard st nw, see Riggs st nw	29	42
Wilson st nw, from Le Droit av to 5th	28	39
Wilberforce st **nw**, fr 622 S to 6th T	25	39
Yale st nw, **fr 11th ext**	20	38

PARKS, Etc.

	M.	T.
Armory sq, fr 6th to **7th bet B** nw and B sw	53	40
Botanic garden, fr 1st to 3d **bet** Pa av nw and Md av sw	53	38
Dupont circle, 19th and P and Mass and Conn avs nw	26	47
Executive Mansion grds, fr Pa av to **B** bet 15th and 17th	47	46
Farragut **sq**, 17th bet I and K	38	43
Franklin **sq**, bet 13th **and** 14th and **I and** K nw	41	44
Garfield **pk, fr S** Cap **to 3d bet** E se	58	34
Iowa circle, intersn **of 13th and** P and Vt and R **I** avs nw	33	43
Judiciary sq, fr 4th and **La avs** to G bet 4th and 5th **nw**	47	40
Lafayette sq, bet Pa av **and H** and 15th and 17th nw	43	46
Lincoln sq, E Cap bet 11th and 13th	51	30
McPherson **sq, 15th bet I and** K nw	41	45
Mt Vernon **pl, K bet 7th and 9th** nw	40	42
Monument grounds, fr 14th bet B **nw** and B **sw**	66	45
Pacific circle, see Dupont circle	26	47
President's pk, see Executive Mansion grounds	47	46
Providence sq, D bet 2d and 3d se	56	35
Rawlins's sq, E **and N Y av** bet 18th and 19th **nw**	48	48
Scott circle, 16th **and N and** Mass and R I **avs nw**	34	45
Seaton pk, bet 3d and **7th, bet** B nw and B sw	52	40
Seward pl, Pa and **N C avs bet** 4th and 6th se	55	33
Sixth st pk, fr 4½ to 6th bet Me and Mo avs	53	40
Smithsonian pk, fr 7th **to** 12th bet B nw and B sw	53	42
Stanton pl, Md and Mass avs fr 4th to 6th ne	44	33
The Mall, fr 6th to 12th bet B nw and **B** sw	52	43
Third st pk, **fr** 3d to 4½ bet Mo and Me avs	53	39
Thomas circle, 14th and M and Vt and Mass avs nw	35	44
Washington circle, 23d and K and Pa and N H avs nw	33	51

HALLS AND BUILDINGS.

	M.	T.
Abner's **hall**, 708 E nw	47	41
Abraham's hall, 233 L sw	64	37
Armory hall, 9th and E nw	48	45
Association hall, 632 Pa av **nw**	50	51
Barbour Law bldg	49	40
Brokes's hall, 2025 [illegible] **nw**	21	51
Beneficial hall, 1111 **18th nw**	26	48
Bethel hall, 1616 M nw	34	36
Blake hall, 229 7th nw	56	41
Brightwood hall, 7th st rd	15	33
Carroll Institute, 922 F **nw**	47	41
Chain bldgs, 1321 and 1323 H nw	43	44
Chancery bldg, 321 4th nw	50	39
Clabaugh hall, 1620 14th nw	27	43
Columbia bldg, 216 4½ nw	50	40
Columbian Law bldg, 416 5th nw	47	40
Corcoran bldg, 15th and Pa av	46	45
Cosmopolitan hall, 8th c E nw	48	41
Cranch bldg, 614 F nw	47	41
Fenton hall, 1108 E nw	47	43
Franklin hall, 9th c D nw	50	40
Friends of Zion hall, 308 G sw	60	38

	M.	T.
Galbraith hall, 428 L nw	40	30
Georgetown University Law bldg, 6th and F nw	46	41
German hall, 606 11th nw	47	43
Glenn Law, 607 La av nw	49	41
Glover bldg, 1419 F nw	46	45
Goddard hall, M nr 30th nw	22	53
Grand Army hall, 9th and D, L nw and e 7th nw	40	42
Green hall, 1710 Pa av nw	43	48
Gunton bldg, 472 La av nw	48	40
Gunton bldg, (new) cor Pa av and 9th nw	48	42
Hooe bldg, 1328 F nw	46	44
Jackson hall, 330 Pa av nw	51	39
Kellogg building, 1414 and 1416 F nw	46	45
Le Droit bldg, 8th and F nw	46	41
Lenox bldg, 7th and G nw	46	41
Lincoln hall, D c 9th nw	47	42
McCauley's hall, 200 Pa av se	54	34
Marini's hall, 914 E st nw	47	43
Masonic hall, 19 e Pa av nw	39	45
Masonic hall, 306 11th nw	47	53
Masonic hall, 1208 32d nw	19	54
Masonic hall, Anacostia	64	26
Masonic hall Va av c 5th se	58	32
Masonic Temple, F c 9th nw	46	42
May bldg, 506 7th nw	46	41
Mechanics' hall, 1739 Pa av nw	42	45
Moore's hall, 306 9th nw	49	42
Mt Vernon hall, 655 N Y av nw	41	41
National Rifles hall, 920 G nw	44	42
National University Law bldg, 1006 E nw	47	42
Nepheth's hall, 212 9th nw	51	42
Norris bldg, 9d F nw	45	40
Odd Fellows' hall, 419 7th nw	47	41
Odd Fellows' hall, 1873 31st nw	23	54
Odd Fellows' hall (colored) 306 11th nw	50	43
Odd Fellows' hall (Navy yard), 830 8th se	56	31
Pacific bldg, 622 F nw	46	41
Phœnix bldg, 504 10th nw	47	43
Saengerbund hall, 708 E nw	41	41
St Cloud bldg, 530 9th nw	46	42
St George's hall, 510 11th nw	46	43
St Joseph's hall, 407 5th nw	41	41
Scottish Rite hall	44	43
Seidham's hall, 1021 7th nw	40	41
Turnverein hall, 306 6th nw	49	39
Vernon row, 945 Pa av nw	49	42
Washington hall, 3d e Pa av se	53	34
Wayland hall, I nr 18th nw	37	39
Webster Law bldg, 503½ D nw	48	40
Willard hall, 1412 F nw	45	45
W L I Corps' hall, 15th and E	48	45

PLACES OF AMUSEMENT.

	M.	T.
Albaugh's Grand Opera House.—15th street, corner E northwest	48	45
Harris' Bijou Opera House.—9th street, below Pennsylvania avenue	50	42
New National Theatre.—E street, between 13th and 14th sts	47	44
Opera House.—Northeast corner D and 9th streets northwest	47	42
Theatre Comique.—11th street west and C street north	51	43
Willard's Hall.—F street rear of Willard's Hotel	46	45

CARRIAGE RATES, Etc.

Rules and Rates of Fare established by law for Hacks, Cabs, or other vehicles for hire in the District of Columbia.

	Between 5 a. m. and 12.30 p. m.	Between 12.30 a. m. and 5 a. m.
For one or two passengers in a one-horse vehicle.	Per hour, 75 cts.; per trip, 75 cts.	Per hour, $1.12; per trip, $1.12.
For one or two passengers, four-seated vehicle drawn by two horses, within the city.	Per hour, $1.50; per trip, exceeding 1 mile, $1.	Per hour, $2.25; per trip, exceeding 1 mile, $1.50.
For one or two passengers, four-seated vehicle drawn by two horses, from Washington to or from Georgetown.	Per hour, $1.50; per trip, exceeding 1 mile, $2.	Per hour, $2.25; per trip, exceeding 1 mile, $3.

And for each additional passenger, 50 cents.

One mile or less, one-half these rates.

One-horse vehicle does not include buggies and phaetons.

In all cases where a vehicle is not engaged by the hour it will be considered as being engaged by the trip.

If there should be an overcharge drive to the nearest police station, where officers in charge will immediately decide the case.

The driver is required by law to present a card containing the above rules to every passenger before or upon entering his vehicle.

Herdic and Hansom Cabs

Are run to any part of the city. Fare, 25 cents, within 1 mile; 75 cents per hour for one passenger; $1 per hour for more than one. Stands—East Capitol front and Pennsylvania avenue and Seventh street northwest.

Street Cars.

Fare for each person on all lines, 5 cents.

Tickets are sold by driver or conductor of all cars, 6 for 25 cents, *good on any line.*

Herdic Coaches.

Fare, 5 cents; 6 tickets for 25 cents.

SKETCH OF THE CITY AND DISTRICT.

The act locating the Capitol of the United States on the banks of the Potomac was passed by Congress at New York, in 1790. The land for the proposed District of ten miles square was ceded to the government by the States of Maryland and Virginia. The exact site for the Capital was decided on by George Washington, with the aid of three Commissioners. The name of it was chosen by the latter, and the plat of the city was made by Major L'Enfant, a French engineer. The government made very advantageous terms with the farmers who owned the land where the city now stands. Congress, which had meantime been sitting at Philadelphia, removed to its new home in 1800.

The growth of the city was at first very slow. The government was by a Mayor, Aldermen, and Councilmen. Up to the outbreak of the civil war the Capital seemed to be a failure. It was unattractive in appearance and the citizens were devoid of enterprise. Congress had long ceased to appropriate money for its improvement. There was talk of removing the Capital farther west—to the centre of the continent—but the war revived its waning fortunes. There was a sudden increase of activity and a vast influx of men and money. During these momentous years the population of the capital averaged a quarter of a million of inhabitants.

Afterwards, however, it was threatened with the same old stagnation. The old local government made an effort to inaugurate a comprehensive system of improvements, but were found to be incompetent. In 1871 Congress, by the advice of prominent citizens, devised a new form of government, consisting of a Governor, Legislative Assembly, and Board of Public Works.

The latter body at once undertook the thorough reconstruction and renovation of the city upon a grand scale.

They undoubtedly laid the foundation for its future unprecedented growth and present advantages of Washington as a residence city, though at the same time they recklessly plunged the city into a huge debt, of more than $20,000,000 which is heavier than it can bear without the aid of Congress. There is the more justice in Congress paying this debt, or a large portion of it, as the obligations were incurred mainly because of its presence and through officers of its appointment.

In 1874, owing to the high-handed methods of the prevailing local administration, called, from its leading spirit and highest officer, "The Shepherd Regime," Congress decided to abolish the whole system of local suffrage, and since then the District of Columbia has been governed by a board of three Commissioners appointed by the President and confirmed by the Senate of the United States.

The people have no votes whatsoever, not even in Presidential elections. This is certainly an anomalous state of affairs to find at the capital of the leading Republic of the world. The system undoubtedly has some advantages, and Congress now pays half of the taxes for the city and District; but it is recalled that the measure was originally a compromise, devised when Congress was greatly puzzled and embarrassed over the large deficits and great confusion in the municipal finances; and, judging from this fact and the complaints which from time to time arise from citizens at being taxed for expenditures which they have no share in making, it is doubtful if the present form of government in vogue here will continue without being changed or essentially modified.

The population of Washington is about two hundred thousand inhabitants, nearly one-third of whom are colored persons. During the past decade it has grown faster than any other city in the United States. In general, its magnificent street area is well paved; its sewerage system is almost perfect and its water supply is one of the best in the world.

PLACES OF INTEREST.

PLACES OF INTEREST.

NOTE.—The places are arranged alphabetically for ready reference. The letters and numerals following the titles refer to the Margin (M.) and Tape (T.) on the Map. (See instructions on preceding pages.)

AGRICULTURAL DEP'T. M. 56. T. 44.

The Department of Agriculture is located about midway between the Smithsonian Institution and the Washington Monument. It was created by Congress in 1862, for the purpose of promoting agricultural knowledge and distributing seeds among the people. Over a million packages are sent out annually. The main building is devoted to offices. An **Herbarium and Taxidermist's Work-shops** occupy the second floor. The **Museum of Agriculture and Industrial Exposition** will be found in the frame annex.

The **Conservatory** is west of the main building. It contains tropical plants and fruits and a grapery in the south wing.

The grounds surrounding the Department are beautifully laid out in terraces, flower-beds, and plant-houses.

The Museum and Conservatories are open till 4 p. m., Saturdays till 3 p. m. (*See List of Illustrations.*)

ALEXANDRIA.

On the right bank of the Potomac, about seven miles below Washington; is reached by railroad from the Baltimore and Potomac depot and by ferry-boats which run every hour in the day; horse-cars on 7th street connect with the ferry. Alexandria was for many years included in the District of Columbia, but has since been ceded back again by the United States to the State of Virginia. It is now devoid of the commercial activity which once characterized it.

Christ Church, in which Washington worshiped, is an old and quaint structure standing near the centre of the town.

ANALOSTAN ISLAND. M. 46. T. 56.

Opposite Georgetown; about 70 acres, not under cultivation; a resort for pleasure excursions.

AQUEDUCT. M. 5. T. 57.

The aqueduct which supplies the city with water is led to its destination by a series of tunnels and magnificent bridges, the largest of which, called the **Cabin-John Bridge**, is considered one of the most successful engineering feats in the world. The material is granite blocks, formed into a single arch, with a span of 220 feet (making it the largest stone bridge in the world); cost $237,000; first projected in 1853; distance from the city, about 12 miles.

ARLINGTON. M. 82. T. 55.

On the right bank of the Potomac, about four miles from the Capitol stands the fine mansion which was at one time the home of General Robert E. Lee. It was purchased by the United States Government in 1864. The drive to it, through Georgetown, is a pleasant one.

THE NATIONAL CEMETERY

embraces about two hundred acres of the old Custis estate on Arlington Heights. The grounds were first formally opened for a soldiers' cemetery by the Government in 1867. 16,000 soldiers are buried here, both Union and Confederate. A portion of the cemetery is reserved for colored troops. Near Arlington House is a granite sarcophagus erected over the bones of 2,111 unknown soldiers, who perished at Bull Run and on other battle fields and in hospitals. By this tomb is a great amphitheater, capable of accommodating the large audience at the memorial exercises which are held here annually in honor of the heroes of the war. (*See List of Illustrations.*)

ARMY MEDICAL MUSEUM. M. 46. T. 42.

Stands on 10th street west, midway between E and F streets, north. The **Museum** on the third floor of the building is very complete. It contains (1) a surgical section (illustrating injuries received from missiles in war, and their treatment); (2) medical section (illustrating camp diseases); (3) microscopical section (illustrating diseased tissues and organs); (4) anatomical section (illustrating human anatomy); (5) section of comparative anatomy (illustrating skeletons of American mammals, birds, and fishes); (6) miscellaneous section (illustrating hospital and barracks life.)

On the first, second, and third floors are **offices of the Surgeon-General and subordinates** and the **hospital records of the Civil War** and those received from present posts of the regular army. **A laboratory** is connected with the establishment.

The building has a peculiar interest from the fact that it was the **scene of President Lincoln's assassination** by Wilkes Booth, April 14th, 1865. It was then Ford's Theater. After the tragedy it was closed by the Government, and in 1866 devoted to the purpose for which it is now used. Lincoln died in a house opposite the Museum. The hours for visitors are from 9 a. m. to 3 p. m.

The new building being erected by the Government in the grounds of the Smithsonian Institution will be ready for occupancy at an early date and will be admirably arranged to contain the collections and library described above. (*See List of Illustrations.*)

ARSENAL: U. S. BARRACKS. M. 71. T. 35.

These grounds are located at the foot of 4½ street S.W., and may be reached by horse-cars. There are quarters for five batteries. The garrison drills daily; the store-houses contain ammunition and arms. **Specimens of guns and mortars** now in service may be seen; also some of those captured in various wars. The hours for visitors are from sunrise to sunset.

BOTANICAL GARDEN. M. 52. T. 38.

The Government Botanical Gardens are bounded by 1st and 3d streets west and Pennsylvania and Maryland avenues. The main entrance is opposite the center of the west side of the Capitol grounds. The gardens are open to visitors from 9 a. m. to 6 p. m. Carriages are not permitted to enter the grounds. The collection of shrubs and flowers contain specimens from many climes.

The **Conservatory** is filled with varieties of palms and other tropical plants, including trees from Japan, China, and Egypt. The **smaller conservatories** are devoted to rare flowers and vines, the orchids being especially complete and beautiful.

North of the Conservatory is the **Bartholdi fountain,** from the Centennial Exposition, supplied from the aqueduct, and throwing a stream of water over sixty feet. It can be illuminated by electricity, and is used at its full capacity on national holidays. (*See List of Illustrations.*)

The object of Congress in keeping the garden is mainly the distribution of plants and seeds. Each member of Congress has at his disposal a specified number of them. The collection was first begun over forty years ago.

BUREAU OF EDUCATION. M. 44. T. 41.

The building rented for this bureau stands on the corner of G and 8th streets N. W., opposite the Patent Office. The several floors are occupied by **offices**, a **library**, and a room for exhibiting **educational apparatus**. Visitors are received at the usual hours.

BUREAU OF ENGRAVING AND PR'NT'G.

M. 58. T. 44.

The Bureau of Engraving and Printing stands on the corner of B and 14th streets S. W. It is open to visitors from 9 a. m. to 2 p. m. **on Saturdays only.** Here a very interesting view may be had of every detail in the process of engraving and printing Government bonds, notes, and stamps. (*See List of Illustrations.*)

CAPITOL.

M. 52. T. 36.

The Capitol of the United States is situated on Capitol Hill, about the center of the city of Washington. It fronts east. Strangers generally enter from the west front, as the principal part of the city is in that direction.

DIMENSIONS.

The Capitol is 751 feet in length and 324 feet at its greatest breadth. It covers an area of three and one-half acres. The central portion of the building is built of yellow sandstone, painted white, from Aquia Creek, Va. The wings are built of white marble from Lee, Mass. The dome is built of iron and is 287 feet in height (above the base line of the east front). It is surmounted by a bronze statue of Freedom, 19 feet in height, modeled by the celebrated American artist Crawford. The dome is reached by a stair-case of 290 steps, and from the top may be had a beautiful and very extensive view.

EXTERIOR.

The north and south fronts of the Capitol are alike. The west front of the Capitol consists of three ornamental porticoes. The eastern and most ornamental front contains a central portico 160 feet wide and two corresponding porticoes 142 feet wide. The sandstone group on the tympanum of the pediment of the central portico represents "The Genius of America." On the southern abutment of this portico is a group representing the "Discovery of America." The corresponding group on the northern abutment represents "Civilization of America." The bronze doors at the top of the steps leading to the central entrance to this front are ornamented with scenes from the discoveries of Columbus, and weigh with their casings over twenty thousand pounds. Statues representing "Peace" and "War" fill the niches to the north and south of these doors respectively. Directly over the door is a basso-relievo representing "Fame" and "Peace" crowning Washington with a laurel wreath.

THE ROTUNDA.

The Rotunda is 95 feet in diameter and 180 feet high (to the top of the canopy). The fresco on the canopy, by Brumidi, an Italian artist, represents the Deification of Washington; the Fall of Tyranny; Agriculture; Mechanics; Commerce; Marine Power, and Arts and Sciences. The frieze of the Rotunda is decorated with scenes from American history. The sides of the room are divided into eight panels. Over the panels are busts of Columbus, Raleigh, Cabot, and La Salle (in order named, beginning on the left of the west door).

Over each of the four doors leading from the Rotunda are alto-relievos representing, (1) The Landing of the Pilgrims on Plymouth Rock; (2) William Penn's Treaty with the Indians in 1686; (3) The Preservation of Captain John Smith by Pocahontas; (4) Conflict between Daniel Boone and the Indians. The large pictures which occupy the eight panels are on the following subjects: (1) Declaration of Independence; (2) Surrender of Burgoyne; (3) Surrender of Cornwallis; (4) Resignation of General Washington; (5) Baptism of Pocahontas; (6) Discovery of the Mississippi River; (7) Landing of Columbus; (8) Embarkation of the Pilgrims.

LIBRARY OF CONGRESS.

The **Library of Congress** is at the end of the hallway which leads from the west door of the Rotunda. It is used by the Senators and members of the House of Representatives, Judges of the Supreme Court, and heads of Departments, as well as by the general public. All persons are permitted to consult books in the library. The collection contains **over half a million books** and nearly a quarter of a million pamphlets. It is the largest collection of books in the United States and **one of the largest collections in the world.** It is increased at the rate of about twenty thousand volumes annually. The Librarian of Congress is registrar of all copyrights issued in the United States.

A new Library building will soon be erected on one of the squares east of the Capitol. *(See List of Illustrations.)*

SUPREME COURT.

At the right of the vestibule leading from the north door of the Rotunda is the **Supreme Court of the United States.** This room was for many years the United States Senate Chamber, where so many famous speeches were delivered. The busts on the walls are of former Chief Justices. The court meets annually in October, and usually continues to sit until May, with occasional adjournments. The public are admitted whenever the court is in session.

SENATE.

At the end of this same hallway is the present United States Senate Chamber. The **main door at the eastern corridor** is a massive paneled piece of bronze representing scenes in the American Revolution, by Crawford.

RECEPTION ROOM.

The Senate Reception Room, at the right of this door, is paved with marble and elaborately frescoed. Adjoining this room, from which visitors' cards are sent in to Senators after two o'clock, are the Senate Post Office and office of the Sergeant-at-Arms of the Senate. The west door of the Reception Room leads to the Lobby of the Senate, which is accessible to visitors when the Senate is not in session. At the right of the Lobby is the Vice-President's Room. Next is the celebrated Marble Room, with sides and floors of polished marble of different tints. Here Senators receive guests by appointment.

GALLERIES.

At foot of the stairs leading to the east gallery of the Senate is the statue of Franklin by Powers, and over the first landing is Powell's noted picture of Commodore Perry's victory over the British on Lake Erie. The east gallery of the Senate is the Ladies' Gallery; the west is the Gentlemen's Gallery; the central portion of the north gallery is for the newspaper reporters; opposite this is the Diplomatic Gallery, for foreign representatives. The Ladies' Retiring-Room adjoins the Ladies' Gallery on the north side. The two large paintings in the vestibule of the Ladies' Gallery—"The Grand Cañon of the Yellowstone" and "The Grand Cañon of the Colorado"—are by Thomas Moran, an American artist.

PRESIDENT'S ROOM.

On the right of the west vestibule is the President's Room, where he sometimes remains to sign bills in the last hours of a session of Congress. This room is handsomely frescoed with symbolical designs and adorned with portraits of American statesmen. At the foot of the staircase leading to the west gallery is a statue of John Hancock, by Stone. "The Storming of Chapultepec under General Scott," which hangs over the first landing, is by the artist Walker.

SENATE CHAMBER.

The Senate Chamber is a well-proportioned room one hundred and twelve feet in length. The desks of the Senators are of polished mahogany. Some of them were used in the old Senate Chamber. The paintings on the skylight represent The Union, The Army, The Navy, etc. Under the east, west, and south galleries are cloak-rooms for the Senators. On this floor and the floors above and below are various committee rooms. The Senate Chamber is heated and ventilated through great registers connected with machinery in the basement.

The Vice-President presides over the sessions of this body on a dais at the north end of the chamber. The public are admitted to the floor when the Senate is not in session. They are admitted at all times to the galleries, excepting when the Senate is in executive session.

BASEMENT OF SENATE.

In the basement of the Senate wing are, besides the **Committee Rooms** (which may be visited on permission from Senators), the **Restaurant, folding rooms,** and the official **telegraph and telephone office**—connecting with the various Departments of the Government and the Government Printing Office.

THE CRYPT.

Beneath the Rotunda, extending toward the Senate, is **The Crypt**, and under this is the **Undercroft**—offered for keeping the remains of George Washington, but refused by his family.

LAW LIBRARY.

Underneath the court-room is the **Law Department of the Congressional Library**, one of the finest technical libraries in the United States. This room was **formerly occupied by the Supreme Court.**

. STATUARY HALL.

The next room south of the Rotunda is the old hall of the House of Representatives. It is now used as a Hall of Statuary, Congress having devoted it to this purpose "in order that each State should send the effigies of two of her chosen sons to be placed here permanently." Rhode Island has sent Roger Williams, "the Apostle of Religious Liberty," and Nathaniel Green, Major General in the Army of the Revolution; Connecticut, Jonathan Trumbull, the last Colonial Governor of the State, an intimate friend of Washington, and Roger Sherman, delegate to Congress and one of the signers of the Declaration of Independence; New York, George Clinton, Vice-President of the United States, and Robert Livingston, a signer of the Declaration of Independence; Massachusetts, John Winthrop and Samuel Adams; Vermont, Ethan Allen, the hero of Ticonderoga, and Jacob Collamer, an early Postmaster General and United States Senator; Maine, William King, her first Governor; Pennsylvania, Robert Fulton, inventor of steam navigation, and Peter Mühlenburgh, a "fighting minister" (General) in the Revolutionary War.

Besides these statues the Government is represented by the following works of art:

Miss Ream's statue of Abraham Lincoln, for which Congress paid ten thousand dollars; bust of Lincoln; bust of Thomas Crawford; statue of Alexander Hamilton; bronze statue of Thomas Jefferson; cast of Washington; bust of Kosciusko; portraits of George Washington, Thomas Jefferson, Charles Carroll, Henry Clay, Gunning Bedford, Benjamin West, and Joshua R. Giddings, and mosaics of Lincoln and Garfield. The graceful marble clock in this room represents History in the Car of Time.

HALL OF REPRESENTATIVES.

The Hall of Representatives, which stands at the opposite end of the building from the Senate Chamber, is

the largest legislative hall in the world, being 140 feet in length, 95 feet in width, and 40 feet high. There are desks for 333 members. The **Republican members sit at the left of the Speaker,** and the **Democrats in the right half of the hall.** The galleries will contain about 1,500 persons. The ceiling of the hall is of iron, with glass panels decorated with the arms of the different States. The **Speaker's chair and desk** are in the middle of the south side of the hall, behind the clerk's desk. On the right and left of this desk respectively are life-size portraits of Washington and Lafayette. In the panel next to the portrait of Lafayette is a painting by Bierstadt representing "The Discovery of the Hudson River." In the corresponding panel next to the portrait of Washington is a companion picture by the same artist, the subject being "The King's River Cañon." Adjoining the picture of the Hudson is a fresco representing "Washington at Yorktown."

The

CORRIDORS, LOBBY, GALLERIES, AND COMMITTEE ROOMS

Of the House are in general arrangement and decorations similar to those of the Senate. The **Members' Reception Rooms** and the **Speaker's Room** are open to the public when the House is not in session. At the **foot of the east staircase leading to the galleries** is a statue of Jefferson by Powers; over the first landing is an equestrian statue of General Scott; above the landing of the eastern staircase is the historic painting of President Lincoln and his Cabinet, entitled "Signing the Emancipation Proclamation," purchased by a New York lady and presented to Congress. At the foot of the west staircase corresponding is a bronze bust of a Chippewa Indian Chieftain. Over the first landing is the great picture "Westward Ho," which cost twenty thousand dollars.

BASEMENT OF THE HOUSE.

The basement of the House wing contains a **Restaurant**, and is arranged for **Committee Rooms**. That used by the Committee of Agriculture is noticeable for elaborate frescoing.

The Speaker presides over the House when it is in session. At his right hand, on a pedestal of marble, is kept the mace—consisting of a number of rods bound together by silvered bands and capped by a globe and eagle. This is his official emblem of authority, and, in the hands of the Sergeant-at-Arms, is used (though rarely) to bring unruly members to order. (*See List of Illustrations.*)

CAPITOL GROUNDS.

Eleven avenues and streets lead to the Capitol Grounds from all sections of the city. The principal **western approach** is by Pennsylvania avenue. At the foot of the steps leading to the first terrace is Story's bronze statue of Chief-Justice Marshall. The marble fish-pond on this terrace was the site of a proposed monument to commemorate the deeds of the American navy.

In the **east park** there are handsome granite and bronze vases for plants. In the middle of this great plaza (which holds the crowds who come to witness the Inauguration ceremonies) is Greenough's colossal statue of Washington, bearing the familiar inscription: "First in War; First in Peace; First in the Hearts of his Countrymen;" words first used by Governor Henry Lee, of Virginia.

On the **north side** of the park, about midway up the hill, there has been placed for the refreshment of visitors a rustic summer-house and drinking-fountain.

The stone tower at the **south side** of the grounds aids in supplying fresh air to the ventilating apparatus in the Hall of Representatives.

The Capitol Grounds were formerly smaller than they are now and were neglected. About ten years ago Congress resolved to enlarge and improve them. Frederick Law Olmstead, the New York landscape architect, has been employed to prepare plans for stone terraces and other ornamental work (now in course of construction), which when completed will render the appearance of the Capitol even more imposing than at present.

CENTRE MARKET. M. 51. T. 41.

Occupies the space between 7th and 9th streets, adjacent to Pennsylvania avenue N. W. It is conducted by an incorporated body and affords the best product available. (*See List of Illustrations.*)

CHRIST CHURCH, M. 57. T. 31.

The **oldest church in the city**, is on G street, between 6th and 7th streets, near the Marine Barracks. It dates from 1800, and used to be attended by personages of prominence in political and social circles of the Capital.

COAST & GEODETIC SURVEY OFFICE. M. 55. T. 36.

The United States Coast Survey office occupies a building on New Jersey avenue, near the Capitol. It is here that the **standard weights and measures of the United States** are regulated. (*See List of Illustrations.*)

COLUMBIAN UNIVERSITY. M. 42. T. 45.

The main building is on the corner of 15th and H streets N. W. It was erected in 1884, and is occupied by the Collegiate and Law Departments. The institution was founded by Baptists in 1822. The President of the United States and the Chief Justice of the Supreme Court are *ex-officio* members of the board of trustees.

CONGRESSIONAL CEMETERY. M. 55. T. 25.

The Congressional Cemetery embraces about thirty acres charmingly situated on the Eastern Branch of the Potomac

River, a mile above the Navy Yard. The act of Congress creating cenotaphs to deceased members has since been repealed. The tract is controlled by Christ Church, which stands near the Marine Barracks. Few congressmen are buried here, but some who died during their term of public service are commemorated by cenotaphs. There are also monuments to a few noted men, among others George Clinton and Elbridge Gerry. The grounds are open every day except Sunday.

CONVENT OF VISITATION. M. 8. T. 55.

On Fayette street, West Washington, near the Catholic College; the grounds are extensive, but are not usually open to visitors.

CORCORAN ART GALLERY. M. 43. T. 47.

The gallery is a well-proportioned building at the corner of Pennsylvania avenue and 17th street. The class of architecture is the Renaissance. On the first floor are a designing room and hall of sculpture. On the second floor are the several picture galleries, containing a large number of very valuable works by American and foreign artists. The collection includes the private gallery of the donor of the building, which was valued at $100,000 at the time of its presentation. The cost of the structure was $250,000. Mr. W. W. Corcoran, the well-known philanthropist of Washington, also bestowed an endowment of $900,000 for supporting his gift, the income of which is expended under the direction of a board of trustees to increase the completeness of the gallery. The purpose of the trust is to afford enjoyment to the public and to promote art. Special facilities are offered to artists wishing to copy works which are on exhibition here. The public are admitted daily between October and May from 10 a. m. to 4 p. m.; between May and October from 9 a. m.

to 4 p. m. **Tuesdays, Thursdays, and Saturdays admission is free**; on other days the charge is 25 cents. (*See List of Illustrations.*)

DEAF-MUTE COLLEGE. M. 41. T. 31.

The National Deaf-Mute College and Columbian Institution for the Deaf and Dumb is at the north end of 7th street east. The grounds, of 100 acres, are known as "Kendall Green." A portion of them were formerly owned by Amos Kendall, when Postmaster-General of the United States. The institution was incorporated by the Government in 1857, and many deaf-mute children of members of the army and navy corps and of residents of the District of Columbia have since received a collegiate education there, free of expense. The main building, which is a handsome and symmetrical stone structure, was dedicated by Congress in 1871. The institution is open every day excepting Sunday.

DEPARTMENT OF JUSTICE. M. 44. T. 45.

Stands opposite the north front of the Treasury, on Pennsylvania avenue. The building was **originally the Freedman's Bank**. The **Attorney-General's office** and the **Court of Claims** against the United States are now located here. In the office of the former is a fine collection of portraits of his predecessors. A very fine law library, including full sets of the Reports of all the States and Territories in the Union, is open to the public.

DISTRICT COURT-HOUSE. M. 48. T. 39.

The District Court-House (formerly City Hall) stands on the south side of Judiciary Square, which extends from the intersection of Louisiana and Indiana avenues to G street, and from 4th to 5th street. The courts of the District of Columbia sit here. The marble **statue of Abraham Lincoln** in front of the building was purchased and placed there by the efforts of private citizens.

DISTRICT GOV'T'S OFFICE. M. 50. T. 40.

Four-and-a-half street, near Pennsylvania avenue. A more commodious office will probably soon be erected.

DUPONT CIRCLE. M. 27. T. 47.

Formed by the intersection of Massachusetts avenue, Connecticut avenue, and other streets and avenues, N. W. The statue of Rear Admiral Dupont is by Launt Thompson, erected in 1884 by Congress.

EXCURSIONS FOR SIGHT-SEERS.

Single trips in the city (in order of interest): I. The Capitol. II. The White House. III. Patent Office. IV. National Museum. V. Bureau of Engraving and Printing. VI. Corcoran Art Gallery.

Single trips outside the city (in order of interest): I. Mt. Vernon. II. Soldiers' Home. III. Arlington Cemetery.

A fine view of the city may be obtained from the top of Messrs. Moses & Sons' high building, corner of 11th and F streets N. W. Elevators run between the hours of 8 a. m. and 6 p. m. Visitors are invited to use them free of charge.

EXECUTIVE MANSION, OR "WHITE HOUSE." M. 46. T. 46.

The "White House" fronts on Pennsylvania avenue, about one mile and a half west of the Capitol. The plan is said to have been copied from an Irish nobleman's country house. The material is sandstone painted white. The dimensions are 180 feet in length by about 90 in in depth. Carriages can drive under the wide portico on the north side. The south front has a semi-circular colonnade of six columns.

The following are the rooms on the first floor: **Vestibule,** 40 by 50 feet; **East Room,** 80 by 40 feet, used for public receptions—the only room in the building at all times accessible to visitors (between the hours of 10 a. m. and 3 p. m.)

Adjoining this apartment, en suite, are the **Green Room**, the **Blue Room**, and the **Red Room.** These rooms take their name from the prevailing tints of their decorations and furniture. The one last named is the room most commonly used by occupants of the house for social purposes. At receptions the President usually receives his guests in the Blue Room. The **State Dining-Room**, where all the large dinners are given, is at the southwest end of the building. The **Family Dining-Room** is just north of this.

On the second floor are the **Executive Offices**, including the **President's Private Room**, in which the Cabinet meetings are held. A library is attached to it. The sleeping apartments have a southern and western frontage.

The **basement** contains the **kitchen, servants' quarters**, and **store-rooms.**

Stables and a **conservatory** are attached to the "White House."

Many of the decorations and furnishings of the Executive Mansion made since 1881 are expensive and beautiful and will repay an effort made to secure from attendants the privilege of examining them in detail.

The "**White House" grounds** contain about eighty acres laid out in walks and drives. Near the south portico is a **band-stand**, from which, on summer evenings, it has been the custom to have the Marine Band play selections for the entertainment of the public. (*See List of Illustrations.*)

FALLS OF THE POTOMAC.

The distance from Georgetown to the **Great Falls** of the Potomac is about 15 miles; the channel of the Potomac River here is narrow and rocky, and there are picturesque cascades. The water with which Washington is supplied is carried from this point, by aqueduct, to an immense receiving reservoir. A steam-packet from Georgetown carries passengers on this excursion.

The "Little Falls" of the Potomac are about four miles above Georgetown. The scenery, though pretty, is not so bold as that at the Great Falls.

FISH-COMMISSION. M. 56. T. 40.

The United States Fish-Commission stands on the corner of B and 6th streets S. W. The appliances on exhibition here appertain to the hatching of varieties of salmon, trout, herring, shad, and other valuable fish. The Commission was created in 1871 and is under the charge of Professor Baird, the well-known specialist, who has made American fish-culture famous throughout the civilized world. The premises can be inspected on week days till four o'clock in the afternoon.

FISH-PONDS. M. 54. T. 46.

A few hundred yards from the Washington Monument are the Government ponds for raising carp and other fish. They were established and are managed by the United States Fish Commission. Persons desiring to stock their ponds are supplied with carp. About 300,000 of them are raised here annually. Gold fish and turtles are also hatched. The premises may be inspected between the hours of 8 a. m. and 4 p. m.

FORT MYER. M. 88. T. 56.

Near Arlington House; used in the Civil War; now a signal station.

FRANKLIN SQUARE. M. 41. T. 44.

Between 13th and 14th and I and K streets N. W.; beautifully laid out with trees, shrubs, and a fountain; was purchased by the Government many years ago for the purpose of controlling a spring to supply the White House with drinking-water.

GEOLOGICAL SURVEY M. 47. T. 45.

Is located in the iron building, 1332 F street. Here are prepared the various scientific reports which have given this branch of the Government a world-wide reputation. The large collections of the Survey may be seen at the National Museum.

GEORGETOWN M. 12. T. 52.

Is now called West Washington. It is the port of entry for the District of Columbia; about two miles north of the White House; is reached by the F street and Pennsylvania avenue lines of horse-cars; was founded many years before the Capital.

GEORGETOWN UNIVERSITY, M. 5. T. 56.

At the head of O street northwest, under the care of Jesuits, is the **oldest Catholic college in the United States,** being founded in 1789. Here is a library of thirty thousand volumes and many old and rare manuscripts. The new stone building is a fine one, open to visitors, excepting Sunday.

GOV'T PRINTING OFFICE. M. 44. T. 37.

This building is situated on the corner of H and North Capitol streets, and should be entered from the door opening on the latter street. The hours are from 8 a. m. till 5 p. m. The printing of Congress and the Departments is done here. It is **one of the largest printing offices in the world,** the outfit including press-rooms, folding-rooms, paper warehouses, electrotyping and stereotyping departments, besides the type-setting and proof rooms. All of the documents distributed by Congress are printed here. The cost of the work amounts to several millions of dollars annually.

GREENE'S STATUE. M. 49. T. 33.

The equestrian statue of General Nathaniel Greene, the well-known Revolutionary general, beautifies Stanton Place, at the intersection of Massachusetts and Maryland avenues N. E. It was erected in 1877 by Congress. *(See List of Illustrations.)*

HOSPITAL FOR INSANE. M. 72. T. 27.

The Government hospital for care of insane persons is on the opposite side of the river from the Navy Yard. It is open to visitors on Wednesday afternoons. The grounds are several hundred acres in extent; are well cultivated and afford a perfect view of the Capital. One thousand persons can be accomodated in the building, which was designed by Walter, architect of the new wings of the Capitol. This institution is for the use of the army and navy and residents of the District of Columbia. It was founded in 1855.

HOWARD UNIVERSITY. M. 24. T. 37.

Howard University commands a fine view of the Capital from a plateau beyond the northern terminus of the 7th-street horse-railroad. The building contains recitation-rooms, a dormitory, library, dining-hall, and offices. There are accommodations for 300 students, residences for teachers, and grounds thirty-five acres in extent, valued, in all, at six hundred thousand dollars. The institution was incorporated in 1867 and named in honor of General Howard, who was then manager of the Freedmen's Bureau. Pupils of either sex or color are admitted to the privileges of the University, though at present attendance is confined almost without exception to the colored race.

LAFAYETTE SQUARE. M. 43. T. 46.

Opposite the White House. The statue of General Jackson in the center of the park was designed by Clark Mills; cost $50,000, and was erected in 1853, on the anniversary of the battle of New Orleans. (*See List of Illustrations.*)

LINCOLN PARK. M. 51. T. 30.

About one mile from the Capitol, at the head of East Capitol Street, between 11th and 13th Streets. The statue and group in honor of Lincoln which stand in the center of the park were donated by freedmen; cost $17,000, and considered among the finest works of art in the city. (*See List of Illustrations.*)

LOUISE HOME M. 34. T. 46.

On Massachusetts avenue, just south of Scott Circle, is a memorial by Mr. W. W. Corcoran to his deceased wife and daughter. Southern ladies needing a home are cared for here. Accommodations for 55 inmates are at the disposal of the board of directors. The building cost $200,000, and the institution is well endowed. Open to visitors in the afternoons.

LUTHER STATUE. M. 35. T. 44.

Just northeast of the Thomas Statue, across the circle, is the bronze statue of Martin Luther, erected, in 1884, by members of the Lutheran Church.

McPHERSON SQUARE. M. 40. T. 45.

On Vermont avenue, between I and K streets N. W. The bronze statue of General McPherson was erected in his honor by the Society of the Army of the Tennessee, of which he was commander in 1864. The material is cannon appropriated by Congress. (*See List of Illustrations.*)

MARINE BARRACKS. M. 57. T. 30.

The Marine Barracks are two squares north of the Navy Yard, on 8th street. There are accommodations for about two hundred men.

The Marine Corps is an adjunct of the Navy Department. Its headquarters are here in Washington. The armory at the Barracks contains some **historic battle-flags.** The premises may be inspected from 9 a. m. till sundown. **Mondays,** at 10 a. m., there is a drill of marines, with **music by the band.**

MOUNT VERNON.

Mount Vernon, for many years the residence of Washington and the site of his tomb, is distant from the Capital about sixteen miles down the Potomac river. Many points of interest may be observed on the sail. The mansion is attractive in appearance, is in an excellent state of preservation, and contains a full collection of household relics and paintings belonging to the illustrious owner of the mansion and his esteemed spouse. The numerous out-buildings on the premises are much as the owner left them. The house itself and grounds are now under care of the "Mount Vernon Ladies' Association of the Union," a society which was incorporated in 1856 for this worthy object. **The tomb** in which the remains of Washington and his wife lie buried is built of brick, with iron gratings, and incloses marble sarcophagi.

Mount Vernon is reached by steamboat W. W. Corcoran, Capt. L. L. Blake, via the 7th street line of horse-cars. The boat starts at 10 a. m. daily, excepting Sundays, and lands passengers in the city at 4 p. m. The fare for the round trip is one dollar, including admission to the grounds.

NAT'L MILITARY CEMETERY. M. 22. T. 27.

Adjoins the Soldiers' Home; opened in 1861; contains the graves of several thousand Union and Confederate soldiers.

NATIONAL MUSEUM. M. 55. T. 41.

Just east of the Smithsonian stands the new National Museum, an immense structure built in 1879, covering over two acres of ground and containing all the collections made on Government exploring expeditions and many other curiosities in nearly every department of the arts and sciences. The halls on the ground floor are en suite, and display the collections of pottery, ceramics, geological specimens, fossils, etc., etc. In the towers and elsewhere are many offices devoted to investigations in osteology, paleontology, metallurgy, and other scientific branches. The necessary funds for them are supplied by the Government. A quarter of a million of dollars was appropriated by Congress to build the Museum. The collections were removed here in 1883. The premises may be visited daily from 9 a. m. to 4 p. m. (*See List of Illustrations.*)

NAVAL HOSPITAL. M. 55. T. 30.

Is situated near the Marine Barracks, between 9th and 10th streets. It is used for the navy and marine corps. Hours for visitors, afternoons of week days.

NAVAL MONUMENT. M. 51. T. 37.

This is one of the most beautiful and effective statues in Washington. It stands on Pennsylvania avenue, at the western approach to Capitol Hill. The name given to it by Congress is "The Monument of Peace." Figures representing "History," "America," "Victory," and "Peace" adorn the top and sides of the shaft. The inscription is to the memory of the officers, seamen, and marines who fell in defense of the Union in the Civil War. The funds were raised by contributions from officers and sailors in the Navy, to which Congress added $25,000 to complete the statue and the pedestal.

NAVAL OBSERVATORY. M. 49. T. 51.

The United States Naval Observatory occupies a prominent position on the bank of the Potomac, at the foot of 24th street. The grounds comprise nearly 20 acres. The group of buildings consist of a main building, with revolving dome (containing an equatorial telescope), and two wings, for residence of the Superintendent, taking observations, etc. There are rooms for a mural circle and transit, chronometer, sidereal clock, and other astronomical instruments. The great Equatorial—the largest in the world—is mounted in a new and commodious extension in the rear of the main building. It cost, with the setting, over $60,000; was made in Massachusetts and weighs in all six tons.

The National Observatory is one of the leading Observatories of the world. It was founded by Congress in 1842. The premises are open daily from 9 a. m. to 3 p. m.

The Government has purchased a site for a new Observatory finely located in Rock Creek valley, and will soon begin construction.

NAVY DEPARTMENT. M. 45. T. 47.

(For description of building see State Department.) In the **Hydrographic Office**, on the basement floor, are made all the charts furnished for the Navy and for commerce. The **Office of the Secretary of the Navy**, on the second floor, is elaborately decorated. The Library, on the fourth floor, is a costly and convenient room, with a good collection of books, for the use of members of the department. Hours for visitors, from 9 a. m. to 3 p. m. (*See List of Illustrations.*)

NAVY YARD. M. 61. T. 30.

The Navy Yard is located on the banks of the Anacostia River, about one mile southeast of the Capitol. It is reached by horse-cars via Pennsylvania avenue, and may be visited during all hours of the day. The grounds comprise about 27 acres, and in them are grouped **ordnance-foundries and gun-shops. A naval storehouse** supplies all the necessaries for fitting out vessels. There is **a museum illustrating naval warfare** which contains several antiques valuable. Officers and men of the marine corps are stationed at this point.

OAK HILL CEMETERY. M. 15. T. 51.

Containing 25 acres; situated on high ground, at the head of 30th street, West Washington. Many distinguished men are buried here, including the author of "Home, Sweet Home."

PATENT OFFICE. M. 45. T. 41.

The Patent Office is bounded by 7th and 9th and F and G streets N. W. The site is the one originally intended for a national church. The older portion of the building is painted sandstone and the new part is white marble. The lower stories are occupied by the **Indian Office, Public Land Office,** and other branches of the Department of the Interior. The **Model Rooms** are on the second floor. They contain models of a great number of patents issued by the Government.

In 1877 a fire destroyed many of the old patent-models. The building has since been handsomely renovated and is now fire-proof. The Patent Office is no expense to the Government, but, on the contrary, yields it a large revenue annually, from the fees received for issuing patents. It is an institution which in its way is unequaled in the world, and of which every American may be justly proud. The models may be seen every week day between the hours of 9 a. m. and 4 p. m. (*See List of Illustrations.*)

PENSION BUILDING. M. 45. T. 39.

The United States Pension Building occupies a conspicuous site on Judiciary Square, north of the District

Court-House. The huge structure covers two acres, is of rather a unique style of architecture, and cost $500,000. The interior hallways look on a court yard of vast dimensions, roofed over and lit with side windows. In this hall the Inaugural ball of 1885 was held, with ten thousand persons in attendance. There are regular accommodations for 15,000 clerks. Hours of admittance, from 9 until 2. (*See List of Illustrations.*)

POST OFFICE (CITY) M. 49. T. 40.

Stands on Louisiana avenue, near the intersection of 7th street and Pennsylvania avenue N. W. Congress has recently taken steps to erect a much more commodious building.

POST OFFICE DEPARTMENT. M. 47. T. 41.

The building is one of the handsomest in Washington; covers the square opposite the Patent Office, between 7th and 8th and E and F streets N. W. It is built of Maryland and New York marbles and is in the Corinthian style of architecture. The proportions are about 200 x 300 feet. In the center is a large court yard faced with granite. The building cost nearly a million and three-quarters of dollars. **The Postmaster-Generals's Office** and the **Dead-Letter Office** are located in this building. The Postmaster General was not admitted to the Cabinet till President Jackson's term of office. The Dead-Letter Office may be visited by permit from the chief clerk in the building. The hours for visiting the department are between 9 a. m. and 3 p. m. (*See List of Illustrations.*)

PROPAGATING GARDEN. M. 58. T. 45.

The Government nursery for trees and shrubs, to supply the public parks with and for forcing and curing flowers and seeds, includes 8 acres of land on the banks of the Potomac river, a short distance southwest of the Bureau of Engraving and Printing.

RAWLINS SQUARE. M. 48. T. 48.

Situated on New York avenue a short distance west of the State Department. The statue of General John A. Rawlins, at one time chief-of-staff to General Grant and subsequently Secretary of War, was erected in 1874, by the combined efforts of Congress and his personal friends.

ROCK CREEK CEMETERY M. 14. T. 44.

Is adjacent to the Soldiers' Home; the site is picturesque, and the church is a very old one, built of bricks brought from England. Services are held here on the Sabbath, and the grounds are open to the public on week days.

ROUTES FOR DAYS.

First day: The Capitol, Navy Yard, Marine Barracks, Government Printing Office, and Botanical Garden.

Second day: White House, Treasury Department, State, War, and Navy Departments, Corcoran Art Gallery, and Naval Observatory.

Third day: Smithsonian Institution, National Museum, Department of Agriculture, Bureau of Engraving and Printing, Washington Monument, and Patent Office.

SCOTT CIRCLE, M. 33. T. 45.

At the intersection of Massachusetts and Rhode Island avenues. The statue of General Winfield Scott is made from cannon captured in the Mexican War; the pedestal is composed of some of the largest pieces of Massachusetts granite ever quarried; ordered by Congress and located in 1874. (*See List of Illustrations.*)

SIGNAL OFFICE. M. 44. T. 47.

This Bureau occupies two brick houses west of the War Department, on G street. Here is the office of the famous "**Old Probabilities,**" whose duty it is to inform the country of the state and indications of the weather. The work was begun in 1871 and has since been much extended and developed. In the **Instrument Room,** on the fourth story, may be seen the apparatus for making the observations. The hours are from 12 m. to 3 p. m.

SMITHSONIAN INSTITUTION. M. 55. T. 42.

The Smithsonian Institution stands in a park of 20 acres, south of Pennsylvania avenue, between 7th and 12th streets. The building is of red sandstone and the architecture is the style usually called Romanesque. The work was completed in 1856, at a cost of nearly half a million dollars. This sum was bequeathed to the United States Government by James Smithson, an English gentleman and a scientist, "to found an establishment for the increase and diffusion of knowledge among men."

The object of the Institution, as now defined, is for scientific research and publication. The current expenses are defrayed by income from the donation. The Regents or governing board are appointed by Congress. In the grounds are a **statue of Professor Joseph Henry**, first Secretary of the Institution, and a **memorial vase** in honor of **Andrew Downing,** the landscape gardener who first improved this park. It has lately been cared for by Congress, and is planted with many varieties of American trees and shrubs. The building is open daily from 9 a. m. to 4 p. m., except Sundays. (*See List of Illustrations.*)

SOCIAL CUSTOMS.

The etiquette of Washington is not so intricate as it is often supposed to be by strangers. Nevertheless there are a few social observancies prevalent here which it will be well for visitors to understand and to follow.

TITLES.

The following titles should be used in conversation with those who bear them: "Mr. President" (to the President of the United States); "Mr. Vice-President" (to the Vice-President of the United States); "Mr. Secretary" (to any of the members of his Cabinet); "Mr. Chief Justice" (to the Chief Justice of the United States); "Mr. Justice" (to the other members of the Supreme Court); "Mr. Speaker" (to the Speaker of the House of Representative); "Senator" (to Senators of the United States); "Mr." (to members of the House of Representatives); their regular titles to officers of the army or navy.

In addressing letters or communications to the above their full title should be used, all members of Congress of course being "Honorable." It is customary in formal letters for the wives to receive the titles of their husbands on their letters, as "Mrs. Secretary of the ——," "The Hon. Mrs. ——," etc., though this rule is not invariable.

RECEPTIONS, ETC.

Most of the social entertainments at the Capital occur between New Years and Lent. The most notable are the public receptions held at the White House and the residences of the members of the President's Cabinet and of the various Senators and Representatives. The dates for holding them are announced in the newspapers soon after the opening of Congress, (on the first Monday in December of each year.) The hours for the receptions are usually from 2 until 5 in the afternoon and from 8 until 11 in the evening. The afternoon receptions are open to the public, and the evening are by card, unless announcement to the contrary is made. The dress appropriate to these occasions is the same as would be worn elsewhere at corresponding hours. It is not necessary to send acceptances to the evening receptions. Cards should be handed to the usher at the afternoon receptions.

CALLING.

The hours for general calling during the season are from 3 until 6 p. m. Evening calls have gone out of style in

Washington recently, excepting between intimate friends. The President and mistress of the White House do not return calls. The wives of Secretaries, Judges, Senators, and Representatives return the visits of their acquaintances when called upon first. The ladies of Judges of the Supreme Court usually receive on Mondays; members of the Cabinet on Wednesdays; Senators on Thursdays and Representatives on Tuesdays.

The President receives visitors daily at half-past one o'clock, excepting on Cabinet days (which are Tuesdays and Thursdays) Saturday and Sunday. Persons are received at other hours by appointment by sending in their cards. Only intimate friends are received at the White House socially in the evening.

These hours are subject to slight change according to the season of the year. Special reception days are selected for different sections of the city and are announced by the press at the beginning of the season.

SOLDIERS' HOME. M. 22. T. 34.

The drive to this place is the favorite one in the vicinity of Washington. The park comprises about 500 acres, finely situated, 4 miles to the northward of the city, and carefully laid out in lawns, gardens, and pathways. The group of houses include a Dormitory, Hospital, Chapel, and residences for the Governor and Surgeon.

Several Presidents of the United States have occupied one of the cottages here in summer. On the brow of the hill, commanding a fine view of the Capitol, is a bronze statue of General Scott, through whose efforts the home was founded shortly after the close of the Mexican War. The sum donated by Congress has since been increased by levying a small monthly tax on each soldier in the regular army. Disabled private soldiers in the army are cared for at the home, free of charge. The grounds are open every day. Horse-cars which approach nearest are the 7th-street line and continuation. (*See List of Illustrations.*)

STATE DEP'T BUILDING. M. 46. T. 47.

This, the largest public department building in Washington, stands west of the White House, fronting Pennsylvania avenue. The dimensions, including steps, are 567 feet x 342 feet. The design was made by Mullett, supervising architect of the Treasury, and is suggestive of the Roman Doric style of architecture. The material is granite from Maine and Virginia. The building was begun in 1871 and has cost over $5,000,000. The **south wing** is occupied by the **Department of State,** the **north wing** by the **War Department,** and the **east wing** by the **Navy Department.** All the offices are substantially and many of them are elegantly furnished. The Diplomatic Reception Room is a particularly sumptuous apartment. The **Library** in the third story of the **State Department** is very complete and valuable, relating principally to the diplomatic history of the United States. Here is preserved also the original Declaration of Independence, and other Revolutionary documents. Open to the public daily between 9:30 and 2:30, excepting Thursdays and Saturdays (during sessions of Congress.) (*See List of Illustrations.*)

THOMAS STATUE M. 36. T. 44.

At the intersection of Massachusetts avenue and 14th street N. W., was designed by the sculptor Ward, and erected to the memory of Gen. George H. Thomas by the Society of the Army of the Cumberland in 1879. Cost, $50,000. (*See List of Illustrations.*)

TREASURY DEPARTMENT. M. 46. T. 45.

The United States Treasury Department stands on 15th

street, a few rods east of the White House. It contains nearly two hundred rooms or offices.

The following are those of most interest to visitors: **Cash Room,** opposite the north entrance, with floor and walls of rare marble; **The Vaults,** built of steel and iron, in which the gold is kept—in the northeast section of the building (about $10,000,000 is usually kept here at one time); the **Secret Service Bureau,** showing counterfeiters' implements and photographs of the criminals; **Office of the Secretary of the Treasury,** a handsome apartment on the second floor, south corridor.

The rooms of the **Supervising Architect of the Treasury** are in the basement and contain plans of the principal buildings erected by the Government. The **Redemption Division,** for canceling, by machinery, money unfit for circulation, is in the north corridor of the same floor. Counting the currency, by lady clerks, may be watched through the doorways of the west corridor, north end.

The Treasury Building cost nearly seven millions of dollars. The portion fronting on 15th street stands on the site of the old Treasury Building, which was burned in 1833. The granite of which it is built was brought from Maine. The design of the building is of Greek (Ionic) architecture. The Treasury Department may be visited daily from 9 a. m. to 2 p. m. (*See List of Illustrations.*)

WAR DEPARTMENT. M. 45. T. 47.

(For description of the building see State Department.) The **Headquarters of the Army** are on the first floor, east of the main entrance. In this room is a collection of portraits of distinguished American generals, battle scenes, and sketches of border life. The **Apartments of the Secretary of War,** second floor, north corridor, contain some fine specimens of tile work. On the third floor is a military library. Hours for visitors, daily, between 9 a. m. and 2 p. m. (*See List of Illustrations.*)

WASHINGTON MONUMENT. M. 56. T. 45.

This structure may be most conveniently approached from Pennsylvania avenue where it turns at the Treasury, thence by 15th or 17th streets. It is also convenient of access from the Bureau of Engraving and Printing. The height of the obelisk from the foundation is 555 feet. This makes it **the highest work of human hands in the world.** Its weight is over 80,000 tons; the base is 55 feet square; the walls are 15 feet thick; the material is Maryland marble; foundation Gneiss rock and Portland cement. The interior of the shaft is hollow, and is furnished with an elevator (not now running) and an iron staircase of 900 steps. The view from the windows at the top of this flight is extensive, both of the city and surrounding country. Tablets adorn the lower portion of the interior of the monument, and it is intended that similar contributions in marble and bronze to the memory of Washington from States, Territories, foreign nations, religious societies, charitable organizations, and similar institutions shall beautify the remaining space. The grounds at the base will also probably be elaborately improved, eventually, with tiling, pathways, etc.

The monument has already cost more than $1,187,000. Three hundred thousand dollars of this was contributed by the society which was incorporated to build the monument and the remainder by the United States Government.

The project of building this memorial was actively begun in 1833 by citizens of the city of Washington, who asked the general public to contribute, and with $87,000 in hand laid the corner-stone of the edifice July 4th, 1848. Work on the shaft ceased in 1855 and was not resumed till 1880. In 1876 Congress appointed a committee to complete the work and made generous appropriations for this purpose; but delay was caused by the necessary precaution of strengthening the old foundations. The dedication of the completed monument occurred on Saturday, February 21st, 1885, with appropriate ceremonies. (*See List of Illustrations.*)

WASHINGTON STATUE. M. 35. T. 51.

At Washington Circle, 23d street W., at the intersection of Pennsylvania and New Hampshire avenues; designed by Clark Mills; voted by Congress in 1853; cost $50,000, and was cast from cannon. Washington is represented as at the battle of Princeton. (*See List of Illustrations.*)

WAYLAND SEMINARY. M. 20. T. 41.

The Seminary overlooks the city from Meridian Hill, a short distance from the northern terminus of the 14th-street horse-railroad. The institution was founded in 1865, by Baptists, to educate colored men for the ministry and for teaching. The building was erected in 1874 by colored labor; cost $35,000, and will accommodate two hundred students.

WINDER'S BUILDING M. 45. T. 47.

Stands opposite the Navy Department, at the corner of F and 17th streets, and is occupied by the **Chief Engineer of the Army**, the **Judge Advocate General of the Army**, **the Battle Record Room**, and the **Ordnance Office**. **The Museum** connected with the latter contains many flags, uniforms, projectiles, and relics of the Civil War, and foreign arms. Visitors are admitted from 9 a. m. till 3 p. m.

NATIONAL GOVERNMENT.

GOVERNMENT OF THE UNITED STATES.

THE EXECUTIVE.

President of the United States—GROVER CLEVELAND, Executive Mansion.
Private Secretary—Daniel S. Lamont, 2024 G n. w.
Assistant Private Secretary—O. L. Pruden, 317 11th s. w.

STATE DEPARTMENT.

17th street below Pennsylvania avenue n. w.

Secretary of State—Thomas F. Bayard, 1413 Mass. ave. n. w.
Assistant—James D. Porter, Riggs House n. w.
Chief Clerk—Sevellon A. Brown, 1500 13th n. w.

Foreign Legations in the United States.

Argentine Republic, 1822 Jefferson place n. w.
Austria-Hungary, 1440 Massachusetts avenue.
Belgium, New York city.
Brazil, 1710 Pennsylvania avenue n. w.
Chili, 1225 N street n. w.
China, Dupont circle n. w.
Colombia, The Hamilton.
Costa Rica, 1714 Pennsylvania avenue.
France, 1340 I street n. w.
Germany, The Portland.
Great Britain, Connecticut avenue, corner N street n. w.
Hawaii, 1330 L street n. w.
Italy, 1340 I street n. w.
Japan, 1310 N street n. w.
Mexico, 1418 K street n. w.
Netherlands, 47 Broad street, New York.
Peru, Hamilton House n. w.
Portugal, 1401 H street n. w.
Russia, 1705 K street n. w.
Spain, 1447 Massachusetts avenue.
Sweden and Norway, 1714 Pennsylvania avenue n. w.
Switzerland, 2031 I street n. w.
Turkey, 1705 K street n. w.
United States of Colombia, 1217 N street n. w.

TREASURY DEPARTMENT.

Pennsylvania avenue, corner 15th street n. w.

Secretary of the Treasury—Daniel Manning, 1501 18th street n. w.
Asst. Secretary—Chas. S. Fairchild, 1347 Connecticut avenue n. w.
Hugh S. Thompson, ——.
Chief Clerk—Edward B. Youmans, 1520 Connecticut ave. n. w.

Supervising Architect's Office.

Supervising Architect—M. E. Bell, 1338 Vermont ave. n. w.
Chief Clerk—Thomas D. Fister, 1507 Rhode Island avenue n. w.

Commissioner of Customs.

Commissioner—John S. McCalmont, 1327 G street n. w.
Deputy—H. A. Lockwood, B street, corner 1st s. w.

Register of the Treasury.

Register—William S. Rosecrans, Willard's Hotel.
Assistant—Roswell A. Fish, 1208 Virginia avenue s. w.

First Auditor.

Auditor—James Q. Chenoweth, 1342 Vermont avenue n. w.
Deputy—E. P. Baldwin, 142 A street n. e.

Second Auditor.

Winder's Building, 17th and F streets n. w.

Auditor—William A. Day, 27 Iowa circle n. w.
Deputy—H. C. Harmon, Howard avenue, Mt. Pleasant (D. C.)

Third Auditor.

Auditor—John S. Williams, 25 Madison place n. w.
Deputy—William H. Welsh, Baltimore, Md.

Bureau of Statistics.

407 15th street n. w.

Chief of Bureau—Wm. F. Switzler, 734 12th street n. w.
Chief Clerk—Joseph N. Whitney, 1827 I street n. w.

Mint.

Director of the Mint—James P. Kimball, 1311 N. H. ave. n. w.

Bureau of Engraving and Printing.

14th street, corner B s. w.

Chief of Bureau—E. O. Graves, 1700 14th street n. w.
Assistant—Thomas J. Sullivan, 1530 9th street n. w.

First Comptroller's Office.

Comptroller—Milton J. Durham, 1331 G street n. w.
Deputy—John R. Garrison, 628 B street n. w.

Second Comptroller's Office.

Comptroller—Isaac H. Maynard, 25 Madison place n. w.
Deputy—Richard R. McMahon, 1729 F street n. w.

Fourth Auditor.

Auditor—Charles M. Shelley, 1507 Rhode Island avenue n. w.
Deputy—Benjamin P. Davis, Mt. Pleasant (D. C.)

Fifth Auditor.

Auditor—Anthony Eickhoff, 607 New Jersey avenue n. w.
Deputy—J. B. Mann, 1010 Massachusetts avenue n. w.

Auditor of the Treasury for the Post Office Department.

Auditor—Daniel McConville, 1414 N street n. w.
Deputy—E. A. Clifford, 1225 New York avenue n. w.
Chief Clerk—Boone Chambers, 603 F street n. w.

Treasurer of the United States.

Treasurer—Conrad N. Jordan, 1537 P street n. w.
Assistant—James W. Whelpley, 800 East Capitol street.
Chief Clerk—James F. Meline, Burnt Mills, Md.

Comptroller of the Currency.

Comptroller—Wm. L. Trenholm, 1913 I street n. w.
Deputy—V. P. Snyder, 1016 15th street n. w.

Commissioner of Internal Revenue.

Commissioner—Joseph S. Miller, 1302 Rhode Island avenue n. w.
Deputy—H. C. Rogers, 1520 S street n. w.

Secret Service Division.

Chief—James J. Brooks, 1020 17th street n. w.

Light-House Board.

President—Daniel Manning, Secretary of the Treasury, ex-officio, 1501 18th street n. w.
Chairman—Vice-Admiral Stephen C. Rowan, U. S. N., Ebbitt House.

Coast and Geodetic Survey,

New Jersey avenue, near B street s. e.

Superintendent—F. M. Thorn, 109 C street s. e.
Assistant in charge of office—B. A. Colonna, 23 Grant place n. w.

Marine Hospital Service.

1421 G street n. w.

Supervising Surgeon General—John B. Hamilton, 9 B street n. w.

Bureau of Navigation.

Commissioner—Jarvis Patten, 1531 P street n. w.
Deputy—T. B. Sanders, 1410 10th street n. w.

WAR DEPARTMENT.

Pennsylvania avenue, corner 17th street n. w.

Secretary of War—William C. Endicott, 1313 16th street n. w.
Chief Clerk—John Tweedale, 901 R street n. w.

Headquarters of the Army.

Lieutenant General—Philip H. Sheridan, 1617 Rhode Island avenue n. w.
Military Secretary—Lt. Col. M. V. Sheridan, 1712 N street n. w.

Adjutant General's Department.

Adjutant General—Brig. Gen. Richard C. Drum, 1516 K street n. w.
Chief Clerk—Raphael P. Thian, 3311 N street n. w.

Inspector General's Department.

Inspector General—Bvt. Maj. Gen. Absalom Baird, 1741 G st. n. w.
Chief Clerk—Warren H. Orcutt, 509 East Capitol street.

Quartermaster General's Department,

Pennsylvania avenue, corner 15th street n. w.

Quartermaster General—Brig. Gen. S. B. Holabird, 1811 P st. n. w.
Chief Clerk—J. Z. Dare, 1340 Corcoran street n. w.

Subsistence Department,

15½ street, near Pennsylvania avenue n. w.

Commissary General of Subsistence—Brig. Gen. Robert Macfeely, 2015 I street n. w.
Chief Clerk—William A. DeCaindry, 1713 H street n. w.

Pay Department,

Pennsylvania avenue, corner 17th street n. w.

Paymaster General—Brig. Gen. William B. Rochester, 1320 18th street n. w.
Chief Clerk—G. D. Hanson, 1228 Massachusetts avenue n. w.

Corps of Engineers,

Winder's Building, 17th street, corner F n.w.

Chief of Engineers—Bvt. Maj. Gen. John Newton, 1327 G st. n.w.
Chief Clerk—William J. Warren, 1234 Massachusetts ave. n.w.

Public Buildings and Grounds,

1700 Pennsylvania avenue n.w.

In charge—Colonel John M. Wilson, 1141 Connecticut ave. n.w.

State, War, and Navy Building, Washington Monument, and Army Medical Museum and Library,

612 17th street n.w.

In charge—Colonel Thos. Lincoln Casey, Corps of Engineers, 1419 K street n.w.
Chief Clerk—Edward Sutherland, 1418 S street n.w.

Ordnance Department,

Winder's Building, 17th street, corner F n.w.

Chief of Ordnance—Brig. Gen. Stephen V. Benét, 1717 I st. n.w.
Chief Clerk—John J. Cook, 927 M street n.w.

Judge Advocate General's Office,

Winder's Building, 17th street, corner F n.w.

Acting Judge Advocate General—Colonel G. Norman Lieber, 1322 18th street n.w.
Chief Clerk—Thomas Duke, 1455 Corcoran street n.w.

Medical Department,

1505 Pennsylvania avenue n.w.

Surgeon General—Brig. Gen. Robert Murray, 1500 I street n.w.
Chief Medical Purveyor—Col. J. H. Baxter, 1504 H street n.w.

Army Dispensary and Office of Attending Surgeon,

1735 G street n.w.

Attending Surgeon—Capt. Robert M. O'Reilly, 1911 I street n.w.
Apothecary—Wm. White, 1813 F street n.w.

Signal Corps,

1725 G street n.w.

Chief Signal Officer—Bvt. Maj. Gen. Wm. B. Hazen, 1601 K street n.w.

Publication Office, War Records,
G street, corner 20th n.w.

In charge—Bvt. Lieut. Col. R. N. Scott, 1721 De Sales st. n.w.

Washington Barracks,
Foot of 4½ streets s. w.

Headquarters 3d Artillery.

Commandant—Colonel Horatio G. Gibson.

NAVY DEPARTMENT.

East Wing of Department Building, Pennsylvania avenue and 17th street n. w.

Secretary of the Navy—William C. Whitney, 1731 I street n. w.
Chief Clerk—John W. Hogg, 1303 R street n. w.

Office of the Judge Advocate General.

Judge Advocate General—Col. Wm. B. Remey 1320 F street n.w.
Lieut. Samuel C. Lemley, 1702 F street n. w.

Bureau of Yards and Docks.

Chief of Bureau—Commodore David B. Harmony, The Portland.

Navy Yard.

Commandant—Commodore Walter W. Queen, Navy Yard.

Bureau of Navigation.

Chief of Bureau—Commodore John G. Walker, 1730 H street n.w.

Naval Observatory,
E between 23d and 24th streets n.w.

Superintendent—Commander Allan D. Brown, 1830 H street n.w.

Nautical Almanac.

Superintendent—Professor Simon Newcomb, 941 M street n.w.

Signal Office.

Chief Signal Officer—Com. Wm. B. Hoff, 1511 20th street n.w.

Hydrographic Office.

Hydrographer—Com. J. R. Bartlett 1836 Jefferson Place n.w.

Bureau of Ordnance.

Chief of Bureau—Commodore Montgomery Sicard, 1417 Massachusetts avenue, n.w.

Bureau of Provisions and Clothing.

Chief Clerk—Louis E. Beall, 1400 K street n.w.

Bureau of Medicine and Surgery.

Chief of Bureau—Surg. General F. M. Gunnell, 600 20th st. n.w.
Assistant—Surg. William K. Van Reypen, 1021 15th street n.w.

Bureau of Construction and Repairs.

Chief of Bureau—Chief Constructor T. D. Wilson, 1631 16th street n.w.

Bureau of Equipment and Recruiting.

Chief of Bureau—Commodore W. S. Schley, 1826 I street n.w.

Bureau of Steam Engineering.

Chief of Bureau—Engineer in Chief Chas. H. Loring, 1334 19th street n.w.

Admiral's Office.

Admiral—D. D. Porter, 1710 H street n.w.

Naval Dispensary.
1744 G street n.w.

In charge—Med. Inspec. Newton L. Bates, 1233 17th street n.w.

Museum of Hygiene.
1744 G street n w.

Medical Director—T. J. Turner, 1206 15th street n.w.

Naval Hospital.
Pennsylvania avenue and 9th street s. e.

In charge—Med. Dir. Albert L. Gihon, Naval Hospital.

Navy Pay Office.
15th corner New York avenue n.w.

Pay Director and Navy Pay Agent—Thos. J. Looker, 1312 30th street n. w.
Chief Clerk—F. V. Walker, 1607 16th street n.w.

Naval Paymaster's Office, Coast Survey Vessels,

137 Corcoran Building.

Paymaster—J. R. Stanton, 2014 Hillyer avenue n. w.
Clerk—H. C. Jordan, 807 H street n.w.

Marine Corps.

Commandant—Colonel C. G. McCawley, headquarters, Marine Barracks.
Surgeon—A. N. Moore, 1626 15th street n.w.

Naval Advisory Board.

President—Capt. W. P. McCann, 1402 Massachusetts avenue n.w.
Secretary—Asst. Naval Constructor F. T. Bowles, 809 14th st. n.w.

Library and War Records.

In charge—James R. Soley, 1834 Jefferson place n.w.

Office of Naval Intelligence.

In charge—Lieut. Raymond P. Rogers, 1832 Jefferson place n.w.

Examining Board of Medical Officers, for Physical Qualifications of all Officers.

Medical Directors—James Suddards, Riggs House; T. J. Turner, 1304 Rhode Island ave. n. w; W. T. Hord, 1702 19th st. n. w.

Retiring Board.

Rear Admiral—
Commodore J. A. Greer, 2010 Hillyer place.
Captain A. W. Weaver, 2819 N street n.w.
Medical Directors J. M. Browne, Portland n.w.; Wm. T. Hord, 3315 P street n.w.

Naval Examining Board.

Commodore J. A. Greer, 2010 Hillyer avenue n. w.
Captain A. W. Weaver, 2819 N street n.w.
Commander J. H. Sands, 3017 O street n.w.

POST OFFICE DEPARTMENT.

E street bet. 7th and 8th st. n.w.

Postmaster General—William F. Vilas, 1329 M street n.w.
Chief Clerk—Thomas E. Nash, 24 Grant place.
First Asst. Postm. Gen.—Adlai E. Stephenson, 25 Madison place.
Second Asst. Postm. Gen.—A. Leo Knott, 1522 Conn. ave. n.w.
Inspection Div.—Chief, John J. Crawford, 1912 I street n.w.
Mail Equip. Div.—Prin. Clerk, Henry L. Johnson, 227 13th st. s.w.
Third Asst. Postm. Gen—A. D. Hazen, 629 G street s.w.

WASHINGTON CITY POST OFFICE.

Louisiana ave. bet. 6th and 7th street n.w.

Postmaster—Frank B. Conger, 1740 N street n.w.
Assistant—Henry Sherwood, 1017 East Capitol street.

The General Delivery and Box Windows are kept open continuously.

The Letter Carriers' window is open from 6 a. m. to 7 p. m., except on Sundays, when it is open from 9 to 10 a. m. and from 6 to 7 p. m.

The Money Order Office is open from 9 a. m. to 6 p. m., except Sunday.

The Registry Division is open from 8:30 a. m. to 6 p. m.

Deliveries by carriers are made in the central and business portion of the city at 7:30 and 10 a. m., 12 m., and 2 and 4 p. m., and in the outside districts at 8 a. m. and 2 p. m.

Collections are made at 5, 8 and 10 a. m., 12 m., and 2, 4, and 7 p. m. Sundays at 5 p. m.

Money Order and Registered letter business may be transacted at Georgetown, East Capitol, and Station C. At Stations D and E letters may be registered, but no money orders issued.

Georgetown Station.

31st above M streets n.w.

Office hours from 6 a. m. to 8 p. m. Sundays, 9 to 10 a. m. and 6 to 7 p. m.

East Capitol Station,

Corner 3d and East Capitol street.

Office hours from 6 a. m. to 8 p. m. Sunday, 9 to 10 a. m. and 6 to 7 p. m.

Section C.

1413 F street n.w.

Office hours 8 a. m. to six p. m.

Section D.

14th, corner Corcoran street n.w

Section E.

426 7th street s.w.

INTERIOR DEPARTMENT.

7th and F streets n.w.

Secretary of Interior—L. Q. C. Lamar, The Portland n.w.
Assistant Secretary—Henry L. Muldrow, Ebbitt House.
David L. Hawkins, 1009 9th street n. w.
Assistant Attorney General—Zachariah Montgomery, 1008 K street n.w.
Chief Clerk and Superintendent—George M. Lockwood, 734 17th street n.w.

General Land Office.

Commissioner—W. A. J. Sparks, 1216 9th street n.w.
Assistant—S. M. Stockslager, 816 15th street n.w.
Chief Clerk—William Walker, 1108 G street n.w.

Pension Office,

F street, between 4th and 5th n.w

Commissioner—John C. Black, 1515 Rhode Island avenue n.w.
Deputies—First, W. E. McLean, 1502 Vermont avenue n.w.; Second, Joseph J. Bartlett, 1319 Corcoran street n.w.
Chief Clerk—D. I. Murphy, 614 M street n.w.

U. S. Pension Agency,

802 F street n.w.

Pension Agent—Sidney L. Wilson, 517 4th street n.w.

Patent Office.

Commissioner—Martin V. Montgomery, 1315 Mass. ave. n.w.
Assistant—Robert B. Vance, 911 Rhode Island avenue n.w.
Chief Clerk—Schuyler Duryee, Falls Church, Va.
Examiners-in-Chief—R. L. B. Clarke, 216 New Jersey avenue s.e.; H. H. Bates, The Portland n.w.; R. J. Fisher, Jr., 1915 Harewood avenue n.w.

Indian Office,

509 7th street n.w.

Commissioner—J. D. C. Atkins, 507 4th street n.w.
Chief Clerk—Alexander B. Upshaw, 1808 16th street n.w.

Office of Education,

G street, corner 8th n.w.

Commissioner—
Chief Clerk—William H. Gardner, 29 5th street n.e.

Geological Survey,

1330 F street n.w.

Director—John W. Powell, 910 M street n.w.
Chief Clerk—James C. Pilling, 918 M street n.w.

Office of the Commissioner of Railroads,

803 G street n.w.

Commissioner—Joseph E. Johnston, 1023 Connecticut ave. n.w.

Bureau of Labor,

1416 F street n.w.

Commissioner—Carroll D. Wright, 1207 T street n.w.
Chief Clerk—Oren W. Weaver, 1005 G street n.w.

Board of Indian Commissioners.

1429 New York avenue n.w.

Chairman—General Clinton B. Fisk.

DEPARTMENT OF JUSTICE.

Pennsylvania avenue, opposite Treasury.

Attorney General—Augustus H. Garland, 1315 Rhode Island ave.
Solicitor General—John Goode, 1600 16th street n.w.
Solicitor and Examiner of Claims, State Department—Francis Wharton, 1607 I street n.w.

AGRICULTURAL DEPARTMENT.

On the Mall, between 12th and 14th street s.w.

Commissioner—Norman J. Colman, 2 Iowa circle n.w.
Chief Clerk—F. C. Nesbit, 2 Iowa circle n.w.

THE SMITHSONIAN INSTITUTION.

Secretary—Prof. Spencer F. Baird, 1445 Massachusetts ave. n.w.
Chief Clerk—Wm. J. Rhees, 1317 11th street n.w.

NATIONAL MUSEUM.

Director—Prof. Spencer F. Baird, 1445 Massachusetts ave. n.w.
Assistant—Prof. G. Brown Goode, Summit ave., Lanier Heights.

U. S. FISH COMMISSION.

1443 Massachusetts avenue n.w.

Commissioner—Prof. Spencer F. Baird, 1445 Mass. ave. n.w.
Assistant—T. B. Ferguson, Richmond Flats.

The Government Carp Pond on the Monument lot and the old Columbia Armory are stations of the Commission.

BUREAU OF ETHNOLOGY.

1330 F street n.w.

Director—J. W. Powell, 910 M street n.w.
Chief Clerk—James C. Pilling, 918 M street n.w.

CIVIL SERVICE COMMISSION.

City Hall building, head 4½ street n.w.

Commissioners—J. H. Oberly; Alfred P. Edgerton, Willard's Hotel; Charles Lyman, 423 M street n.w.
Secretary—R. D. Graham, 612 18th street n.w.

GOVERNMENT PRINTING OFFICE.

Public Printer—S. P. Rounds, 2001 R street n.w.
Chief Clerk—Cadet Taylor, 1624 15th street n.w.
Assistant Chief Clerk—W. H. Collins, 912 Pennsylvania ave. s. e.
Disbursing Clerk—John Larcombe, 1817 H street n. w.
Foreman of Printing—Henry T. Brian, 34 I street n.w.
Superintendent of Folding-Room—Thomas B. Penicks, 618 L street n.w.
In Charge Congressional Record—Aven Pearson, Globe House, 1201 F street n.w.
Foreman of Binding—James W. White, 512 3d street n.w.

THE NATIONAL BOARD OF HEALTH.

1410 G street n.w.

President—James L. Cabell, M. D.
Vice President—Stephen Smith, M. D.
Secretary—W. P. Dunwoody, 30 Grant place n.w.

JUDICIARY.

SUPREME COURT OF THE UNITED STATES.

Capitol Building.

Chief Justice Morrison R. Waite, 1415 I street n.w.
Justice Samuel F. Miller, 1415 Massachusetts avenue n.w.
Justice Joseph P. Bradley, 201 I street n.w.
Justice Stephen J. Field, 21 1st street n. e.
Justice Samuel Blatchford, 1432 K street n.w.
Justice John M. Harlan, Rockville, Md.
Justice Wm. B. Woods, 1421 K street n. w.
Justice Stanley Matthews, 1800 N street n.w.
Justice Horace Gray, 1721 Rhode Island avenue n.w.
Clerk—James H. McKenney.
Deputy—Charles B. Beall, 1621 13th street n.w.
Marshal—John G. Nicolay, 212 B street s. e.

COURT OF CLAIMS.

1509 Pennsylvania avenue n.w.

Chief Justice William A. Richardson, 1739 H street n.w.
Judge Charles C. Nott, 826 Connecticut avenue n.w.
Judge Glenni W. Scofield, Riggs House.
Judge Lawrence Weldon, Hamilton House.
Judge John Davis, 1211 Connecticut avenue n.w.
Chief Clerk—Archibald Hopkins, 1826 Massachusetts avenue n.w.

MUNICIPAL GOVERNMENT.

THE DISTRICT GOVERNMENT.

COMMISSIONERS.

President—William B. Webb, 1800 F. st. n.w
Samuel E. Wheatley, 1314 30th st. n.w.
Col. William Ludlow, U. S. A., Metropolitan Club.
Secretary—Wm. Tindall, cor. Oakland ave. and Conn. ave. extended

The District Officers.

Assts. to Eng. Com.—Capt. T. W. Symons, Lieut. Eugene Griffin.
Attorney—A. G. Riddle, 1116 13th st. n.w.; office 460 La. ave.
Col. of Taxes—John F. Cook, 1005 16th st. n.w.
Assessor—Robert P. Dodge, 1534 28th st., West Washington.
Auditor—I. S. Tichenor, 1211 M st. n.w.
Coroner—De Witt C. Patterson, M. D., 919 I st. n.w.
Surveyor—William Forsyth, 1707 G st. n.w.
Inspector of Buildings—Thomas B. Entwisle, 3057 N st. n.w.

THE DISTRICT JUDICIARY.

Criminal Court—District Court—Common Law Court—Equity Court.

Chief Justice David K. Cartter, 1505 H st. n. w.
Associate Justice William M. Merrick, 1716 N st. n.w.
Associate Justice Arthur MacArthur, 1201 N. st. n.w.
Associate Justice A. B. Hagner, 1818 H st. n. w.
Associate Justice Walter S. Cox, 1636 I st. n. w.
Associate Justice Charles P. James, 1824 Massachusetts ave. n.w.
Clerk—R. J. Meigs, 302 New Jersey ave. s. e.
U. S. Marshal—Albert A. Wilson, 2000 G st. n.w.
Deputy—George W. Phillips, 2 Cooke place n.w.
District Attorney—Augustus S. Worthington, 2015 Mass. ave. n.w.
Assistants—Hugh T. Taggart, 1237 29th st. n.w.; Randolph Coyle, 2806 Q st. n.w.; Fleming J. Lavender, 915 N. Y. ave. n.w.
Register of Wills—H. J. Ramsdell, 2013 Q st. n.w.
Assistant—M. J. Griffith, 1401 5th st. n.w.
Recorder of Deeds—Frederick Douglass, Cedar Hill (D. C.)
Deputy—Geo. F. Schayer, 1318 30th st. n. w.

Police Court.

Corner 6th and D streets n.w.

Judge—Wm. B. Snell, 941 K street n. w.
Clerk—Howard L. Prince, 419 Spruce street, Le Droit Park.
Deputy—Joseph Harper, 113 3d street n. e.
Asst. U. S. Attorney—Fleming J. Lavender, 915 N. Y. ave. n. w.
Special Asst. Attorney for D. C.—J. E. Padgett, 468 La. ave.
Messenger—N. C. Harper, 113 3d street n. e.

THE METROPOLITAN POLICE.

Headquarters 501 D street n.w.

Major and Supt.—Samuel H. Walker, 5th and D sts. n. e.
Captain and Inspector—M. A. Ausitn, 1125 New Jersey ave. n. w.
Station Houses—*First Precinct*, E st. bet. 4½ and 6th sts. s.w.
Second Precinct, U st., bet. 9th st. and Vt. ave. n.w.
Third Precinct, High st., Georgetown.
Fourth Precinct, K st., bet. 20th and 21st sts. n.w.
Fifth Precinct, 12th st., bet. C and D sts. n.w.
Sixth Precinct, 5th st., bet. M and N sts. n.w.
Seventh Precinct, N. J. ave., bet. D and E sts. n.w.
Eighth Precinct, S. C. ave., bet. 5th and 6th sts. s.e.

COUNTY JAIL.

19th and B streets s. e.

Warden—John S. Crocker.
Deputy Warden—Benton Russ.

WASHINGTON ASYLUM.

Intendant—W. H. Stoutenberg.

THE FIRE DEPARTMENT.

Chief Eng.—Joseph Parris, 1129 19th st. n.w.
Asst. Chief Eng. (acting)—Louis P. Lowe, cor. 26th and N sts.
Asst. Chief Eng. (acting)—Charles Merillat, 289 N. Cap. st.
Secretary—Otto C. Reinecke, 428 M st. n.w.
Fire Marshal—Wm. O. Drew, 1337 30th st. n.w.
Engine House—No. 1, K st. bet. 16th and 17th sts. n.w.
No. 2, D st., near 12th st. n.w.
No. 3, Del. ave. and C st., n. e.
No. 4, Va. ave., bet. 4½ and 6th sts. s.w.
No. 5, High st., near Bridge, W. Wash.
No. 6, Mass. ave. bet. 4th and 5th sts. n.w.
No. 7, R st., bet. 9th and 10th sts. n.w.
Truck A, N. Cap., near C st. n. e.
Truck B, N. H. ave. and M st. n.w.

THE COLUMBIA INSTITUTION FOR THE DEAF AND DUMB.

President—Edward M. Gallaudet, Kendall Green.
Secretary—Robert C. Fox, 2013 R street n. w.

The National Deaf-Mute College.

President—Edward M. Gallaudet.

The Kendall School.

Principal—James Denison.

THE FIRE ALARM TELEGRAPH.

First District—Northwest.

12. Second and F streets.
13. Second and H streets.
14. Third and G streets.
15. Mass. ave. bet. 4th and 5th sts.
16. Sixth and B (B. & P. depot) sts.
17. 4½ bet. Pa. ave. and C street.
18. Pa. ave. bet. 3d and 4½ streets.
19. Police station, 1st and F streets.
121. Headquarters, Fifth and D sts.
123. Sixth and G streets.
124. Seven and Louisiana avenue.
125. Seventh and E streets.
126. General Post-office.
127. Seventh and I streets.
128. Ninth and D streets.
131. Ninth and F streets.
132. Ninth and H streets.
134. Medical Museum, 10th street.
135. Eleventh and G streets.
136. Twelfth and L streets.
137. Cor. 10th and New York ave.
142. Thirteenth and F streets.
143. Thirteenth and I streets.
145. Ebbitt House.
146. Riggs House.
147. Fifteenth and I streets.
148. Fourteenth and Vermont ave.
149. L bet. 15th and 16th streets.
151. D bet. 12th and 13th streets.
152. Tenth and C streets.
153. Thirteenth and B streets.
154. Fifteenth and E streets.

Second District—Northwest.

21. New Jersey ave. and K street.
23. Fourth st. and New York ave.
24. Fourth and O streets.
25. Sixth street and New York ave.
26. Fifth and N streets.
27. Fifth st. and Rhode Island ave.
212. Seventh and M streets.
213. Seventh and R streets.
214. Seventh and Boundary streets.
215. Ninth and L streets.
216. Tenth and N streets.
217. Ninth and P streets.
218. Police station, U bet. 9th & 10th.
219. Eng. House No. 7, R. bet. 9th & 10th
231. Eleventh and O streets.
232. Twelfth and Q streets.
234. Twelfth and S streets.
235. Twelfth and V streets.
241. Fourteenth st. and R. I. av.
243. Fourteenth and Corcoran sts.
245. Fourteenth and U streets.
246. Fourteenth and Boundary sts.
247. Sixteenth and P streets.
248. W bet. 12th and 13th streets.
249. Fifteenth near S street.
251. R bet. 16th and 17th streets.
253. Sixteenth and T streets.
254. Nineteenth and R streets.
256. Columbia road and Oakland av.
257. Fourteenth street, cor. W st.

Third District—Northwest.

31. Seventeenth, bet. F and G sts.
32. G, bet. 17th and 18th streets.
34. K, bet. 16th and 17th streets.
35. Sixteenth and M streets.
36. Nineteenth and F streets.
37. Nineteenth st. and Penn. ave.
38. Police Station, K near 20th st.
39. Nineteenth and L streets.
312. Twenty-second and E streets.
314. Twenty-first and H streets.
315. New Hampshire ave. and M st.
318. N, bet. 17th and 18th street.
319. Twentieth and P streets.
321. Twenty-fourth and G streets.
324. Penn. ave., bet. 23d and 24th sts.
325. United States Observatory.
327. Twenty-sixth and I streets.
328. Twenty-fifth and M streets.

Fourth District—Southwest.

41. Maryland avenue and 4½ street.
42. Va. ave., bet. 4½ and 6th sts.
43. Four-and-a-half and B streets.
45. Four-and-a-half and N streets.
46. Arsenal guard house.
47. Police Station, E near 4½ street.
412. Seventh st. and Maryland ave.
413. Seventh and F streets.
415. Seventh and K streets.
416. Twelfth and Water streets.
417. Fourteenth and C streets.
421. National Museum.
423. Eleventh st. and Maryland ave.
425. C bet. Second and Third sts.
426. First and N streets.
427. Sixth, near M street.
431. Thirteenth and C streets.
432. Fourteenth and B streets.
435. Ninth and H streets.
436. Tenth street and Virginia ave.

FIFTH DISTRICT—SOUTHEAST.

51. U. S. Coast Survey, N. J. avenue.
52. Second and East Capitol streets.
53. Second and C streets.
54. Third and L streets.
56. Police Station, 5th and S. C. ave.
512. Seventh and East Capitol sts.
513. Seventh and Pennsylvania ave.
514. Navy-yard gate.
516. Third and B streets.
517. Third and D streets.
521. Eleventh and B streets.
523. Eleventh and I streets.
524. Thirteenth and E streets.
526. Eleventh and M streets.
527. Almshouse.
528. Insane Asylum.

SIXTH DISTRICT—NORTHEAST.

61. No. 3 Eng. H., Del. ave. and C sts.
62. Government Printing Office.
63. Delaware avenue and K street.
64. Deaf and Dumb Asylum.
65. Truck A House, North Capitol st.
67. H, bet. Second and Third sts.
612. Fourth and C streets.
613. Sixth and H streets.
621. Tenth and H streets.
623. North Capitol and F streets.
625. North Capitol and P streets.
627. Eighth and Maryland avenue.
628. Fourteenth and H streets.
631. Sixth and A streets.
632. Ninth and A streets.

SEVENTH DISTRICT—WEST WASHINGTON.

71. Thirtieth and M streets.
72. Thirty-eighth and O streets.
73. Thirty-second and Q streets.
76. Industrial Home School.
712. Thirty-fourth and O streets.
713. Frederick and Seventh streets.
714. Thirty-first and O streets.
723. No. 5 Engine, M near 32d.
731. Thirtieth and K streets.
732. Water and Potomac streets.
735. P street car stables.

THE HEALTH DEPARTMENT,

Office Department Building, 502 D street n.w.

Health Officer—Smith Townshend, M. D., 221 4½ st. n.w.
Chief Clerk—J. C. McGinn, 225 4½ st. n.w.
San. Inspec.—T. W. Parsons, 1306 Corcoran st. n.w.
E. H. Hume, 121 E. Cap. st.
Thomas M. Sheppard, 411 3d st. n.w.
C. H. Welch, 3316 N street n.w.
A. J. Heird, Brightwood, D. C.
B. G. Pool, 1422 11th st. n.w.
Food Inspec.—T. M. Embrey, 1127 9th st. n.w.
J. R. Mothershead, 925 C st. n.w.
Inspec. Marine Products—Gwynn Harris, 218 8th st. s.w.
Pound Master—Samuel Einstein, 221 4½ st.
Physicians to Poor—R. A. Pyles, Anacostia, D. C.
Henry Darling, Brightwood, D. C.
J. H. Yarnall, 3120 N st. n.w.
R. A. Neale, 1909 Penn. ave. n.w.
Peter Goolrick, 718 12th st. n.w.
Louis K. Beatty, 128 11th st. s. e.
R. T. Holden, 802 6th st. s.w.
B. M. Beall, 1740 14th st. n.w.
A. A. Marsteller, 304 C st. n.w.
Edgar Janney, 12 Iowa Circle n.w.

LOCAL ORGANIZATIONS.

LOCAL ORGANIZATIONS.

MILITARY.

Adjutant General, Amos Webster; Chief of Staff, Col. Robert I. Fleming; Engineer, Major H. L. Cranford; Surgeon, Major J. F. Hartigan; Major J. P. Willett and Major H. D. Cook, Aide-de-Camps.

Washington Light Infantry Corps, armory 15th and E street n.w.; Lieut. Col. Wm. G. Moore, commanding; Company A, Capt. W. N. Dalton; Company B, Captain B. R. Ross; Company C, Captain J. C. Entwisle; Company D, Captain J. S. Miller.

National Rifles, 920 G street n.w.; Captain, James F. Oyster; 1st Lieut., J. O. Manson; 2d Lieut., George W. Evans; additional 2d Lieut., W. C. Keech.

National Rifle Cadets, armory 920 G street n.w.; Captain, C. S. Domer.

Union Veteran Corps (Old Guard), organized April 9, 1880; armory 486 Louisiana avenue n.w.; Captain S. E. Thomason.

Union Veteran Corps, armory 7th street, corner L n.w.; Captain M. A. Dillon.

Emmet Guards, armory 4½ street, cor. Pennsylvania avenue n.w.; Captain W. H. Murphy.

Washington Continentals, armory 318 8th street n.w.; Captain William W. Mills.

Corcoran Cadet Corps, armory 510 11th street n. w.; Captain Eugene C. Edwards.

Arthur Rifles, 13th street, corner Pennsylvania avenue n.w.; Lieut. Col., H. W. Rollins; Company A, Captain John C. Pelham; Company B, Captain G. F. D. Rollins.

Light Battery A, Washington Artillery, Captain A. P. Cunningham.

President's Guard, Captain George A. Armes.

Colored Troops.

Washington Cadet Corps, armory 708 O street n. w.; Major C. A. Fleetwood, commanding; Company A, Captain Arthur Brooks; Company B, Captain Richard W. Davidge; Company C, Captain W. H. Lee.

Butler Zouaves, Captain C. B. Fisher.

Capital City Guards, armory 1218 E street n.w.; Lieut. Col., T. S. Kelly, commanding; Adjutant, J. Frank Boston; Company A, P. B. Meredith, Captain; Company B, James A. Perry, Captain; Company C, Jno. H. Campbell, Captain.

Webster Rifles, 1020 20th street n.w.; Captain P. H. Simmons.

Grand Army of the Republic.

National headquarters: Commander-in-Chief, Samuel S. Burdett, 9th and D streets n.w.

Headquarters Department of the Potomac, Grand Army of the Republic, Grand Army Hall, 9th street, corner D n.w., 3d floor.

Posts.

No. 1—John A. Rawlins, 9th and D streets; 2d and 4th Fridays.
No. 2—Kit Carson, 9th and D streets; 2d and 4th Wednesdays.
No. 3—Lincoln, 7th and L streets; 1st and 3d Wednesdays.
No. 4—O. P. Morton, 6th street, cor. C; 2d and 4th Thursdays.
No. 5—Geo. G. Meade, 7th and L streets; 1st and 3d Fridays.
No. 6—John F. Reynolds, 9th and D streets; 1st and 3d Fridays.
No. 7—James A. Garfield, 7th and L sts.; 2d and 4th Wednesdays.
No. 8—Burnside, 7th and L streets; 2d and 4th Thursdays.
No. 9—Charles Sumner, 9th street, cor. D; 2d and 4th Wednesdays.
No. 10—Farragut, 9th street, corner D; 1st and 3d Tuesdays.

Associated Survivors of the War of 1812 of the District of Columbia, formed 18th of June, 1856; headquarters, 1203 H street n.w.

Associated Veterans of 1846, meet at 621 H street n.w.; Recorder and Corresponding Secretary, A. M. Kenaday, lock-box 37.

National Association Veterans of the Mexican War; President, James W. Denver, Washington, D. C.; Secretary, A. M. Kenaday, lock-box 37.

BANKS.

Bank of Washington, 7th street, cor. C n.w.; President, Edward Temple; Discount day, Tuesday; Cashier, Chas. A. James.

Central National Bank, corner 7th and Louisiana avenue; President, Samuel Norment; Cashier, John A. Ruff.

Citizens' National Bank of Washington, D. C., 615 15th street, opposite Treasury Department; capital, $500,000; President, J. A. J. Creswell; Cashier, T. C. Pearsall.

Farmers' and Mechanics' National Bank of Georgetown, 3072 M street n.w.; President, Henry M. Sweeney; Cashier, William Laird, Jr.

German-American National Bank, 632 F street n.w.; Receiver, R. C. Keyser.

National Bank of the Republic, 318 7th st. n.w.; capital, $200,000; President, Dr. Daniel B. Clarke; Cashier, Charles S. Bradley.

National Metropolitan Bank, 15th street, opposite Treasury Department; capital, $300,000; President, J. W. Thompson; Cashier, G. H. B. White; Discount day, Wednesday.

National Savings Bank, District of Columbia, corner 15th street and New York avenue n.w.; President, Benjamin P. Snyder; Vice-President, Lewis Clephane; Secretary and Treasurer, Albert L. Sturtevant.

Second National, 509 7th street n w; capital, $225,000; President, M. G. Emery; cashier, H. C. Swain.

SAFE DEPOSIT COMPANIES.

The National Safe Deposit Company, corner New York avenue and 15th street n.w.; Board of Managers: President, Benjamin P. Snyder; Vice-President, Charles C. Glover; Secretary, Albert L. Sturtevant; Assistant Secretary, C. E. Nyman; Treasurer, Henry A. Willard.

The Washington Safe Deposit Company of Washington, D. C., 916 Pennsylvania avenue n.w.; President, John T. Lenman; Vice-President, James L. Barbour; Secretary and Treasurer, Samuel Cross.

RAILROADS, STEAMSHIPS, AND TRANSPORTATION LINES.

Alexandria and Fredericksburg Railroad, 6th street, cor. B n. w.

Alexandria Canal, Railroad, and Bridge Co., office 1306 13th street n. w., pres., H. H. Wells, sec., W. W. Dungan.

Baltimore and Ohio Railway, N. J. avenue near C street n. w., and 619 Pa. avenue n. w., and 14th street, corner Pa. avenue n. w.; general agent, J. F. Legge.

Baltimore and Potomac Railroad Co., 6th street, corner B n. w., 13th street corner Pa. avenue n. w.; general agent, George C. Wilkins; superintendent, H. H. Carter.

Chesapeake and Ohio Railway, office 513 Pa. avenue n.w. northeastern passenger agent, Frank Trigg.

CLYDE LINE, between New York, Philadelphia, Alexandria, and Washington, D. C., and connects at Philadelphia for Boston and Providence; J. H. Johnson & Co., foot 12th street s.w.; leave Washington every Monday.

KNOX'S EXPRESS AND FAST FREIGHT, 2d street, corner B, and 603 Pa. avenue n.w.

NORTHERN CENTRAL RAILROAD, ticket office Pa. avenue, corner 13th street n.w.

PENNSYLVANIA CENTRAL RAILROAD, ticket office Pa. avenue, corner 13th street n.w.

SOUTHERN MARYLAND RAILROAD Co., office 410 5th street n.w.; president, John Van Riswick; vice-president J. H. Linville, Phila.; treasurer, Frank Hume; chief engineer, J. L. Meigs; secretary and solicitor, T. A. Lambert.

VIRGINIA MIDLAND RAILWAY, office 610 Pa. avenue; president, A. S. Buford; general passenger agent, Mercer Slaughter, Richmond, Va.; agent, N. Macdaniel, Washington, D. C.

WASHINGTON AND CHESAPEAKE RAILROAD, office 413 6th street n.w.; president, S. Taylor Suit; treasurer, John C. New; secretary, Geo. T. May.

WASHINGTON CITY AND POINT LOOKOUT RAILROAD, 413 6th street n.w.; president, S. T. Suit; vice-president, A. W. Dimock; secretary and treasurer, George E. Dimock; chief engineer, W. J. Wharton.

INLAND AND SEABOARD COASTING CO., OF THE DISTRICT OF COLUMBIA, office 6th-street wharf; president, John W. Thompson; vice-president, Samuel Norment; sec. and treas. Alfred Wood; superintendent, George R. Phillips; agent, John M. Williams, foot 6th-street wharf.

MT. VERNON LINE, steamer W. W. Corcoran, foot 7th street s.w.; leaves daily at 10 a. m., returning at 3.30 p. m.

POTOMAC STEAMBOAT CO. (lessee), foot 7th street s.w.; steamers George Leary and Excelsior; gen'l superintendent and agent, William P. Welch.

POTOMAC TRANSPORTATION LINE for Alexandria, river landings, and Baltimore; steamer Sue leaves every Sunday at 4 p. m. from Stephenson's wharf, foot 7th street s.w.

STEAMER MATTANO leaves 7th-street wharf Sundays, Tuesdays, and Thursdays at 7 a. m. for Potomac river landings; agent, G. Tucker Jones.

WASHINGTON STEAMBOAT CO. (limited), foot of 7th street s.w.; manager, C. W. Ridley; treasurer, Jonathan P. Crowley; boats leave hourly from foot of 7th street for Alexandria and return from sunrise to sunset.

STEAMERS ARROWSMITH AND WAKEFIELD for Potomac river landings, daily, 7 a. m.

NEWSPAPERS.

THE EVENING STAR, 1101 Pa. avenue; published daily, except Sunday, by The Evening Star Newspaper Co.; pres., Geo. W. Adams; vice-president, Crosby S. Noyes; secretary and treasurer, S. H. Kauffmann.

THE DAILY NATIONAL REPUBLICAN, Pa. avenue, corner 10th and D streets n.w.; published every morning, Sunday excepted, by The National Republican Co.; E. W. Fox, president and manager; the Weekly Republican, a single sheet of four pages and 32 columns, is published on Thursday.

THE WASHINGTON POST, corner 10th and D streets n. w.; published every morning in the year by the Washington Post Publishing Co.; Stilson Hutchins, editor; weekly edition published every Wednesday.

THE WASHINGTON CRITIC, 941 D street n. w.; published every day except Sunday at the office of the Washington Critic; pres., Hallet Kilbourn; sec., Richard H. Sylvester.

WASHINGTON JOURNAL, 7th street corner G n. w.; published tri-weekly by Werner Koch.

THE REPUBLIC, Thomas H. Heath, manager; published every Sunday morning at 432 9th street n. w.

THE SUNDAY HERALD AND WEEKLY NATIONAL INTELLIGENCER, 403 10th street n. w.; published every Sunday morning; I. N. Burritt, editor and proprietor; T. B. Kalbfus, publisher.

WASHINGTON CHRONICLE, 432 9th street n. w.; J. Q. Thompson, editor and proprietor.

THE CAPITAL, 1420 Pennsylvania avenue n. w.; Edmund Hudson, editor and publisher; published every Sunday morning.

THE SUNDAY GAZETTE, 935 D street n. w.; published by T. G. Morrow every Sunday morning.

DER VOLKS TRIBUN, 804 E street n. w.; German weekly; published every Saturday by E. Waldecker, publisher; Carl Roesser, editor.

ARMY AND NAVY REGISTER, 1420 Pennsylvania avenue n. w.; published Friday; Edmund Hudson, editor and publisher; terms $3.00 per annum.

THE ARMY AND NAVY LIST (Hudson's), monthly, 1420 Pennsylvania avenue.

THE COURT RECORD; published daily at 519 7th street n. w.

THE GAZETTE OF THE PATENT OFFICE; published every Tuesday at the Patent Office.

THE HATCHET; published every Sunday morning at 407 10th street n. w.

THE LAW REPORTER; published every Tuesday morning at 631 F street.

THE PUBLIC OPINION; published every Saturday at 900 Pennsylvania avenue.

THE UNITED STATES GOVERNMENT ADVERTISER; published every Thursday at 1420 Pennsylvania avenue.

LIBRARIES.

There are libraries in all the Departments of the Government, accessible to the employes. The aggregate number of volumes in the city, including the following, is over 900,000.

The Library of Congress occupies the west front of the central Capitol building.

Carroll Institute Library, 602 F street n. w.; number of volumes 3,000.

The Peabody Library, 3233 O street n. w.; librarian, Frank D. Johns.

The Young Men's Christian Association, 1409 New York avenue n. w., has a library of its own numbering 1,200 volumes. The use of the library is free to all members of the Association.

Odd Fellows' Library Association. The library has 5,000 volumes; Odd Fellows' Hall. Secretary and librarian, Z. W. Kessler. Open every night except Saturday.

HOSPITALS, ASYLUMS, &c.

Hospitals.

Government Hospital for the Insane. The site of this hospital is about two miles due south of the Capitol, on the southeast side of Anacostia river. W. W. Godding, M. D., superintendent.

Children's Hospital of the District of Columbia, W street, between 12th and 13th streets n. w. Board of directors: president, Samuel V. Niles; vice-president, M. W. Galt.

Columbia Hospital for Women and Lying-in Asylum, corner 25th street and Pennsylvania avenue n. w. President, G. J. Lydecker; vice-presidents, J. T. Mitchell, Esq., Gen. E. D. Townsend; secretary, L. W. Ritchie, M. D.

The Emergency Hospital established in connection with the Central Dispensary, 416 10th street n.w., is open at all hours of the day and night for the reception and treatment of all accidents and cases requiring immediate attention

Freedman's Hospital and Asylum situated on square between 5th and 7th and Boundary and Pomeroy streets n.w. All classes of patients received without distinction of sex or color. Dr. C. B. Purvis in charge.

Garfield Memorial, Boundary, opposite 10th st. n.w. Resident Physician, William M. Sprigg.

National Homœopathic Hospital, N street, corner of 2d street n.w. President of board of trustees, E. S. Hutchinson

Washington Eye and Ear Infirmary, 1325 H street n.w. Surgeon in charge, F. B. Loring, M. D; assistant, William Nicholson, M. D.

Providence Hospital, 2d and D streets s. e., under the charge of the Sisters of Charity; Sister Beatrice, superior; M. F. Cuthbert, M. D., resident physician.

Asylums.

St. Joseph's Male Orphan Asylum, H street, between 9th and 10th n.w; under the charge of the Sisters of the Holy Cross.

St. Vincent's Female Orphan Asylum, 10th and G streets n.w.; under charge of the Sisters of Charity.

St. Ann's Infant Orphan Asylum, founded August, 1860, K corner 24th street n.w.

The Church Orphanage Association of St. John's parish, of Washington, D. C., 525 20th street. President, Rev. William Paret, bishop of the diocese; warden, Rev. William A. Leonard.

German Orphan Asylum, Good Hope road. Board of directors: president, L. Kettler; vice-president, Charles Graff; matron, Rosanna Obermeyer; superintendent, Charles Obermeyer.

Washington City Orphan Asylum, corner 14th and S street n. w. Board of managers: 1st directress, Mrs. S. P. Lee; 2d directress, Mrs. William M. Merrick.

Homes.

Soldiers' Home is located on Rock Creek Church road, at intersection of Harewood road, covering about 500 acres. Brevet Major Gen. Henry J. Hunt, U. S. A., governor; Capt. Robert Catlin, U. S. A., deputy governor.

Aged Women's Home, 1255 32d street n. w. Mrs. B. Kennon, president; Mrs. J. B. Nourse, secretary.

Colored Widows' Home, St. Matthews' parish, 1909 R street n.w.

Epiphany Church Home for Aged Women, 1319 H street n. w. President, Rev. Samuel H. Giesy, D. D.; vice-president, J. H. C. Coffin.

Home for the Aged, of the Little Sisters of the Poor, corner H and 3d streets n. e. Dr. Raymond T. Holden, physician in charge.

Industrial Home School, 32d street extended n. w. Officers: president, Chas. E. Foster; superintendent, W. S. Stockbridge; matron, Mrs. Emily Stockbridge.

Lenthall Home for Widows, corner 19th and G streets n. w.

Louise Home, corner Massachusetts avenue and 15th street n.w. President, Mrs. John Marbury; secretary, Miss Mary B. Jones; matron, Miss Lucy Hunter.

National Association for the Relief of Destitute Colored Women and Children, 8th street above Grant avenue n. w. President, Mrs. S. C. Pomeroy; vice-president, Mrs. J. B. Bruce.

Reform School of the District of Columbia, Bladensburg road. Geo. W. Adams, president; Geo. A. Shallenberger, supt.

St. Rose's Industrial School, branch of St. Vincent's Female Orphan Asylum, 2023 G street n. w. Sister Clara in charge.

Dispensaries.

Central Dispensary, 416 10th street n. w.; open daily from 1 to 3 p. m. Sundays excepted.

Homœopathic Dispensary, 700 G street n.w; open every day except Sunday from 2 to 4 o'clock p. m.

Women's Dispensary, 925 10th street n. w., open daily, except Sunday, from 2 to 4 p. m; medical and surgical diseases of women and children treated free; Attending Physician, Jeannette J. Sumner, M. D.

CHURCHES.

Baptist.

Calvary, corner 8th and H streets n. w.; Rev. Samuel H. Greene, pastor, 1114 10th street n. w. Memorial chapel, corner 5th and P streets n. w., M. M. Shand, supt.; Kendall chapel, corner 13½ and D streets s. w., H. G. Jacobs, supt.

E-Street, E street near 6th n. w.; Rev. D. W. Faunce, D. D.

Fifth, D street near 4½ s. w.; Rev. C. C. Meador.

First, 13th street, between G and H n. w.; Rev. James H. Cuthbert, D. D.

Gay-street, of Georgetown, corner 31st and N streets n. w.; Rev. J. L. Lodge.

Metropolitan, corner A and 6th streets n. e.; Rev. W. M. Ingersoll.

Mount Tabor, Tenallytown; Rev. Chas. Teasdale.

North, 14th street, between R and S n. w.; Rev. N. J. Wheeler.

Queenstown, Bunker Hill road.

Second, Virginia avenue and 4th street s. e.; Rev. Edmond Hez Swem.

Colored.

Abyssinia, corner 10th and V streets n. w.; Rev. John W. Valentine.

Berean, 18th street, between L and M n. w.; Rev. William Waring.

Bethesda, 2728 M street n. w.; Rev. —— Davis.

Bethlehem, Nichols avenue, Hillsdale; Rev. Henry Scott.

Beulah (old school), corner 3d and P streets n. w.; Rev. John Bell.

Central, corner 3d street n. w.; Rev. John William Roane.

Enon, C street, between 6th and 7th s. e.; Rev. Peter Lewis.

Fifth, Vermont avenue, between P and Q streets n. w.; Rev. John H. Brooks.

First Georgetown, corner Dumbarton avenue and 27th street n. w.; Rev. Sandy Alexander.

First Union, Sherman avenue n. w.; Rev. Augustus A. Watts.

Fourth, R street, between 12th and 13th n. w.; Rev. Robert Johnson.

Israel, corner A and 7th streets n. e.; Rev. Madison Lewis.

Liberty, 1743 E street n. w.; Rev. Edward Willis.

Macedonia, Hillsdale; Rev. Lucius Harrod.

Mt. Carmel, K street, between 4th and 5th n. w.; Rev. H. V. Plummer.

Mt. Hall, 16th street, between B and C n. e.; Rev. Noah Jackson.

Mt. Hermon, 323 23½ street n. w.; Rev. Randolph Peyton.

Mt. Jezreel, 5th and E streets s. e.; Rev. Temple S. Robinson.

Mt. Olive, 1128 6th street n. e.; Rev. Robert Robinson.

Mt. Vernon, Montello; Rev. Horace K. Johnson.

Mt. Zion, 12th and E streets n. e.; Rev. Noah Dillard.
Nineteenth-street, corner 19th and I streets n. w.
North, Meridian Hill; Rev. Peter Lucas.
Pilgrim, 48 O street n. w.; Rev. William H. Campbell.
Rehoboth, 1322 1st street s. w.; Rev. Henry Bailor.
Rock Creek, Tennallytown; Rev. Noah Dillard.
Salem Mission, 1706 N street n. w.; Rev. James Robinson.
Second, 3d street, between H and I n. w.; Rev. M. H. Gaskins.
Seventh, 19th street, between R and S n. w.; Rev. John H. Winston.
Shiloh, L street, between 16th and 17th n. w. Rev. William J. Walker.
South Washington First, 705 6th street s. w.; Rev. William H. Lee.
Third, N street, between 4th and 5th; Rev. Albert Bouldin.
Third, 432 Franklin street; Rev. William R. Jefferson.
Virginia Avenue, 6th street and Virginia avenue s. w.; Rev. R. Laws.
White Oak Branch, 1438 Madison avenue n. w.; Rev. Fielding Robinson.
Zion, 335 F street s. w.; Rev. William Gibbons.

Catholic.

Church of the Immaculate Conception, corner 8th and N streets n. w.; Rev. S. F. Ryan.
Holy Trinity, 36th street n. w.; Rev. Stephen A. Kelly.
St. Aloysius, North Capitol and I streets n. w.; Rev. E. McGwirk.
St. Ann's, Tennallytown; Rev. John T. McCall.
St. Dominick's, 6th and E streets s. w.; Rev. E. Donnelly.
St. Joseph's, 2d and C streets n. e.; Rev. J. P. M. Schleuter.
St. Mary's German, 5th street near H n. w.; Rev. Francis J. Tewes.
St. Matthew's, H and 15th streets n. w.; Rev. P. L. Chapelle, D. D.
St. Patrick's, 10th street, between F and G n. w.; Rev. J. A. Walter.
St. Peter's, 2d and C streets s. e.; Rev. G. W. Devine.
St. Stephen's, Pennsylvania avenue and 25th street n. w.; Rev. John McNally.
St. Theresa, Washington and Fillmore streets, Anacostia; Rev. T. M. Hughes.

COLORED.

St. Augustine's, 15th street, between L and M n. w.; Rev. Michael T. Walsh.

Christadelphian.

Washington Ecclesia, McCauley's Hall, Pennsylvania avenue, between 2d and 3d streets s. e.

Congregational.

First, 10th and G streets n. w; Rev. J. E. Rankin.

Tabernacle of the Congregation (Independent), 9th street, between B street and Virginia avenue, s. w.; Rev. Robert Nourse.

COLORED.

Lincoln Memorial, 11th street, corner R n.w.

Plymouth, 18th street, near L n.w.; Rev. Wm. T. Peel.

Disciples of Christ.

Vermont Avenue Christian, Vermont avenue, between N and O streets n.w.; Rev. Frederick D. Power.

Episcopal.

Ascension, Massachusetts avenue and 12th street n.w; Rev. J. H. Elliott, D.D.

All Saints, Bennings; Rev. John B. Williams.

Christ, G street, between 6th and 7th streets s. e.; Rev. Charles D. Andrews.

Christ, O street, corner 31st n.w.; Rev. Albert R. Stuart.

Church of the Epiphany, G street, between 13th and 14th n.w.; Rev. Dr. Giesy.

Epiphany Mission, 1216 Maryland avenue s. w.; Rev. Irving McElroy.

Emanuel, Washington street, Anacostia; Rev. John M. E. McKee.

Grace, 1029 32d street n.w.; Rev. S. H. Griffith.

Grace, D and 9th street s.w.; Rev. J. W. Phillips.

Holy Cross, Massachusetts avenue, corner 18th street n.w.; Rev. James A. Harrold.

Free Methodist.

637 Massachusetts avenue n.w.; Rev. A. H. Lee.

First, 11th street, between G and I s. e.; Rev. A. H. Lee.

Friends.

Friends' Meeting, Orthodox; Chapel of the Y. M. C. A., New York avenue n w.

Friends' Meeting House, I street, between 18th and 19th n. w.; John F. Dorsey.

Hebrew.

Adas Israel Congregation, Orthodox, 6th street, corner G n.w.; Rev. L. Stern.

Washington Hebrew Reform Congregation, 8th street, between H and I n.w.

Lutheran.

Church of the Fatherland, 6th and F streets n.w.; Rev. A. Homrighaus.

Church of the Reformation, Pennsylvania avenue, corner 2d s. e.; Rev. W. E. Parsons.

Concordia, 20th street, corner G n.w.; Rev. Martin Kratt.

Emanuel, 6th street bet. L and M n.w.; Rev. Louis H. Schneider.

Evangelical, Q street, corner 32d n.w.; Rev. G. A. Nixdorff.

Grace, 13th street, corner Corcoran n.w.; Rev. E. G. Tressel.

Memorial, 14th street, corner Vermont ave. n.w.; J. G. Butler.

St. Johannis, (German Evangelical,) 318 4½ street s.w.; Rev. Earnest Lehnert.

St. Paul's English, 11th st., corner H n.w.; Rev. S. Domer, D. D.

Trinity, 4th street, corner E n.w.; Rev. W. C. A. Luebkert.

Methodist Episcopal.

Edward G. Andrews, D. D., Bishop of the Methodist Episcopal churches, Richmond Flats.

Anacostia, Jackson and Pierce, Anacostia; Rev. C. O. Cook.

Calvary, 35th street, corner T n.w.; Rev. Daniel Haskell.

Dunbarton Avenue, 3133 Dunbarton avenue; Rev. W. S. Edwards.

Fletcher Chapel, 4th street and New York avenue n.w., branch of Wesley Chapel; Rev. W. H. Laney.

Foundry, corner G and 14th sts. n.w.; Rev. Henry R. Naylor.

Fourth Street, 4th street, between E and G s.e.; Rev. M. F. B. Rice.

Gorsuch, 4½ and L streets s.w; Rev. E. D Owen, D. D.

Grace, corner 9th and S streets n.w.; Rev. W. T. L. Weech.

Hamline, corner 9th and P streets n.w.; Rev. J. A. Price.

Little Falls, Canal road; Rev. George M. Berry.

McKendree, Massachusetts avenue, near 9th street n.w.; Rev. C. H. Richardson.

Memorial Chapel, 11th and H sts. n.e.; Rev. Chas. T. House.

Metropolitan, corner 4½ and C sts n.w.; Rev. John P. Newman.

Mount Zion, cor. R and 15th streets n.w.; Rev. Dr. Dashiel.

Mount Zion, Tennallytown; Rev. George M. Berry.

North Capitol, K street, corner North Capitol; Rev. C. T. Weed.

Piney Grove, Anacostia road near Bennings station.

Ryland Chapel, D street cor. 10th s.w.; Rev. Wm. H. Chapman.

Twelfth street, 12th and E streets s.e.; Rev. Thomas Myers.

Trinity, cor. 10th and G streets n.w.; Rev. John W. Valentine.

Union Chapel, 20th st. nr. Pa. avenue; Rev. C. W. Baldwin.

Waugh Chapel, 3d and A streets n.e.; Rev. R. W. Beer.

Wesley Chapel, 5th and F streets n.w.; Rev. Richard Morris.

Colored.

A. M. E. North Mission, Sherman av.; Rev. Samuel Johnson.

Allen's Chapel, Good-Hope road; Rev. John F. Lane.

Asbury, corner K and 11th streets; Rev. Richard A. Reed.

Asbury Mission, 967 Boundary; Rev. Singleton R. Hughes.

Bennings, Bennings D. C.; Rev. Stephen Tasco.

Bethel A. M. E., 26th street, cor. P n.w.; Rev. John L. Davis.

Central, I street near 19th n.w.; Rev G. T. Wright.

East Washington A. M. E., 14th and C streets n.e.; Rev. John H. Turner.

Miscellaneous.

Whitney Avenue Union Mission, Whitney avenue near 7th-st. road; John B Johnston.

Seamen's Bethel Retreat, corner 8th and L streets s.e.; Rev. Samuel Kramer.

Presbyterian.

Assembly's, cor. 5th and I streets n.w.; Rev. George O. Little.

Bethany Chapel (branch of N. Y. avenue church), 13th and C n.w.; Rev. Ward Batchelor.

Central, I street corner 3d n.w.; A. W. Pitzer, D. D.

Eastern, 8th between F and G streets n.w.; Rev. Eugene Peck.

First, 4½ bet. C and D streets n.w.; Rev. B. Sunderland, D. D.

Fourth, 9th between G and H streets n.w.; Rev. Jos. T. Kelly.

Gurley Chapel, Boundary, between 6th and 7th streets n.w.; Rev. Ward Batchelor.

Metropolitan, 4th street corner B s.e.; Rev. John Chester, D. D.

New York Avenue, N. Y. avenue bet. 13th and 14th streets n.w.; Rev. William Alvin Bartlett, D. D.

North, N between 9th and 10th streets n.w.; Rev. Charles B. Ramsdell.

Presbyterian Chapel, 1618 33d street n.w., used for Sunday school; John Leetch, superintendent.

Sixth, 3th street corner C s.w.; Rev. F. H. Burdick, D. D.

Unity, 1630 14th n.w.; Rev. G. B. Patch.

Western, H bet. 19th and 20th sts. n.w., Rev. T. S. Wynkoop.

Westminister, 7th bet. D and E sts. s.w.; Rev. B. F. Bittinger.

West Street, P near 31st street n.w.; Rev. Thos. Fullerton, D. D.

Colored.

Fifteenth Street, 15th bet. I and K streets n.w.; Rev. C. H. A. Bulkley.

Reformed.

First Reformed Trinity, 6th street corner N n.w.; Rev. August Guenther.

Grace Reformed church of the U. S., corner 15th and O n.w.; Rev. C. F. Sontag.

Swedenborgian.

New Jerusalem, North Capitol street near B; Rev. Jabez Fox

Unitarian.

All Souls, 14th and L n.w.; Rev. Rush R. Shippen.

Universalist.

Church of Our Father, 13th street corner L n.w.; Rev. Alexander Kent.

SECRET AND BENEFIT SOCIETIES.

FREE AND ACCEPTED MASONS.

Halls.

Masonic Temple, corner of 9th and F streets n.w.

Masonic Hall, Navy Yard, Virginia avenue, between 4th and 5th streets, east.

Masonic Hall, first ward, corner 19th and Penna. avenue n.w.

Masonic Hall, Georgetown, 32d above M street.

Masonic Hall, Anacostia, Harrison near the bridge.

Brightwood Hall, Brightwood.

Scottish Rite Hall, southwest corner of D and 7th streets n.w., entrance on D street.

Grand Lodge.

Grand Lodge of F. and A. M. of the District of Columbia, meets at Masonic Temple, F street, corner 9th, on the second Wednesday in May and November and 27th of December at 6 p. m. Officers: M.W. Grand Master, T. P. Chiffelle; R. W. G. Sec., W. R. Singleton.

Lodges.

Federal No. 1, meets at Masonic Temple, 2d and 4th Tuesdays.

Columbia No. 3, meets at Masonic Temple, 1st and 3d Wednesdays.

Naval No. 4, meets at Masonic Hall, Navy Yard, 1st Saturday in each month.

Potomac No. 5, meets at Masonic Hall, Georgetown, 1st and 3d Mondays.

Lebanon No. 7, meets at Masonic Temple, 1st and 3d Fridays.

New Jerusalem No. 9, meets at Masonic Hall, 2d and 4th Tuesdays.

Hiram No. 10, meets at corner of 19th and Pennsylvania avenue 1st and 3d Fridays.

St. John's No. 11, meets at Masonic Temple, 2d and 4th Fridays.

National No. 12, meets at Masonic Temple, 1st and 3d Tuesdays.

Washington Centennial No. 14, meets at Masonic Temple, 1st and 3d Thursdays.

Benjamin B. French No. 15, meets at Masonic Temple, 1st and 3d Mondays.

Dawson No. 16, meets at Masonic Temple, 2d and 4th Mondays.

Harmony No. 17, meets at Masonic Temple, 2d and 4th Thursdays.

Acacia No. 18, meets at Masonic Temple, 2d and 4th Tuesdays.

Lafayette No. 9, meets at Masonic Temple, 1st and 3d Thursdays.

Hope No. 20, meets at Masonic Temple, 2d and 4th Fridays.

Anacostia No. 21, meets at Anacostia, 1st and 3d Mondays.

George C. Whiting No. 22, meets at Masonic Hall, Georgetown, 2d and 4th Thursdays.

Pentalpha No. 23, meets at Masonic Temple, 1st and 3d Mondays.

Stansbury No. 24, meets at Masonic Hall, Brightwood, 2d and 4th Mondays.

Arminius No. 25 (works in German,) meets at Masonic Temple, 2d and 4th Mondays.

Royal Arch.

Grand Royal Arch Chapter of the District of Columbia meets at Masonic Temple on the 2d Wednesdays in June and December. M. E. G. H. Priest, G. E. Corson.

Chapters:

Columbia No. 1, meets at Masonic Temple, 1st and 3d Wednesdays.

Washington No. 2, meets at Masonic Temple, 2d and 4th Thursdays.

Mt. Vernon No. 3, meets at Masonic Temple, 2d and 4th Mondays.

Eureka No. 4, meets at Masonic Temple, 2d and 4th Fridays.

Lafayette No. 5, meets at Masonic Temple, 1st and 3d Tuesdays.

Washington Naval No. 6, meets at Masonic Hall, Navy Yard, 3d Tuesdays.

Mt. Horeb No. 7, meets at Masonic Hall, Pennsylvania avenue, corner 19th street, 1st and 3d Thursdays.

Potomac No. 8, meets at Masonic Hall, Georgetown, 2d and 4th Tuesdays.

Knights Templar.

Washington Commandery No. 1 meets at Masonic Temple, on 2d and 4th Wednesdays and on Good Friday.

Columbia Commandery No. 2 meets at Masonic Temple, 1st and 3d Fridays.

Potomac Commandery No. 3 meets at Masonic Hall, Georgetown, 1st and 3d Wednesdays.

DeMolay Mounted Commandery No. 4 meets at Masonic Temple, 2d and 4th Tuesdays.

Scottish Rite.

Supreme Council 33° Southern Jurisdiction of the U. S., 433 3d street n.w.; Secretary General, William M. Ireland.

Mithras Lodge of Perfection No. 1, A. A. S. R., meets in Scottish Rite Hall, 7th and D streets n.w., on the 1st and 3d Tuesdays in each month.

Evangelist Chapter, Knights Rose Croix No. 1, A. A. S. R., meets in the Scottish Rite Hall, 7th and D streets n.w., on the 2d Wednesday in each month.

Robert DeBruce Council of Kadosh meets in the Scottish Rite Hall, 7th and D streets n.w., on 4th Wednesday in each month.

Albert Pike Consistory meets in Scottish Rite Hall, 7th and D streets n.w., on the 2d Tuesdays in February, May, August and November.

Royal Order of Scotland.

Provincial Grand Lodge for U. S. meets annually; Grand Secretary, W. M. Ireland; office, 433 3d street n. w., Washington, D. C.

Miscellaneous.

Masonic Veteran Association; Secretary, W. M. Ireland; meets at Supreme Council offices, 433 3d street n.w., on January 23d.

INDEPENDENT ORDER OF ODD FELLOWS.

R. W. Grand Lodge of the District of Columbia meets in Odd Fellows' Hall in semi-annual session on the second Wednesday of January and July; Grand Secretary, P. Hall Sweet.

Central No. 1 meets every Friday in Odd Fellows' Hall, 7th street n.w.

Washington No. 6 meets every Tuesday in Odd Fellows' Hall, 7th street n.w.

Eastern No. 7 meets every Friday in Odd Fellows' Hall, 7th street n.w.

Harmony No. 9 meets every Monday in Odd Fellows' Hall, Navy Yard.

Columbia No. 10 meets every Thursday in Odd Fellows Hall, 7th street n.w.

Union No. 11 meets every Monday in Washington Hall, Pennsylvania avenue, corner 3d street s. e.

Friendship No. 12 meets every Thursday at 2004 I street n.w.

Covenant No. 13 meets every Monday in Odd Fellows' Hall, Georgetown.

Beacon No. 15 meets every Monday in Odd Fellows' Hall, 7th street n.w.

Metropolitan No. 16 meets every Friday in Moore's Hall, 9th street, near Pennsylvania avenue n.w.

Excelsior No. 17 meets every Monday in Odd Fellows' Hall, 7th street n.w.

Mechanics' No. 18 meets every Friday in Odd Fellows Hall, Georgetown.

Oriental No. 19 meets every Thursday in Odd Fellows' Hall, 7th street n.w.

Federal City No. 20 meets every Wednesday in Odd Fellows' Hall, 7th street n.w.

Golden Rule No. 21 meets every Tuesday at 7th-street Hall n.w.

Encampments.

The Grand Encampment of the District of Columbia meets in Odd Fellows' Hall, 7th street n.w., on the 3d Tuesday in January, July, and November; Grand Scribe, Joseph Burroughs.

Columbia No. 1 meets 2d and last Wednesdays in Odd Fellows' Hall, 7th street n.w.

Magenenu No. 4 meets 2d and 4th Fridays, at Odd Fellows' Hall, Navy Yard.

Mt. Nebo No. 6 meets 1st and 3d Wednesdays, at Odd Fellows' Hall, 7th street n.w.

Fred. D. Stuart No. 7 meets 2d and 4th Tuesdays in 7th-street Hall.

Degree of Rebekah.

Naomi No. 1 meets in Moore's Hall, 309 9th street n.w., 1st and 3d Mondays in each month.

AMERICAN LEGION OF HONOR.

Grand Council meets on the 3d Thursday of February. Grand Commander, M. W. Wines, Coast and Geodetic Survey Office; Grand Secretary, Edward F. O'Brien, 621 P street n.w.

GOOD TEMPLARS.

Grand Lodge meets annually on the 3d Wednesday in November; quarterly in February, May, and August. M. P. Caldwell, G. W. C. T., 511 12th street n.w.; J. H. Bony, G. W. Secretary, 1129 Park Place n.e.

INDEPENDENT ORDER OF MECHANICS.

Grand Lodge of D. C. meets in January and July of each year.

Relief Association.

President, W. L. Seward; Vice-President, Edward Journey; Secretary, J. W. Carter; Treasurer B. T. Trueworthy. Meets 1st Monday at 624 5th street n.w.

INDEPENDENT ORDER OF RECHABITES.

High Tent Independent Order of Rechabites of North America meets annually in May. Columbia District Tent No. 2 meets in February and August of each year. D. C. R., Benj. C. McQuay; D. Sec., Edmund Burke.

INDEPENDENT ORDER OF RED MEN.

Great Council meets in regular session on the second Monday in January, April, July, and October at 1023 7th street n.w.

KNIGHTS OF PYTHIAS.

Grand Lodge Knights of Phythias meets 4th week in January and July. A. N. Thompson, Grand Chancellor; Richard Goodhart, Grand Secretary.

Endowment Rank.

Office of supreme secretary of the Endowment Rank, 916 I street n.w.; Halver Nelson, Supreme Secretary.

SONS OF JONADAB.

Sovereign Council of the World meets annually. Grand Council of District of Columbia meets quarterly, G. C., John Tyler, Jr.

MISCELLANEOUS SOCIETIES.

Agricultural and Horticultural.

District of Columbia Horticultural Association meets in German Hall on 4th Wednesday of each month.

Fruit Growers' Association meets 1st Tuesday in every month.

Art Societies.

Corcoran Gallery of Art; President J. C. Welling, LL. D.; Secretary and Treasurer, Anthony Hyde. Pennsylvania avenue corner 17th street n.w.

Washington Art Club, Vernon Row.

Boat Clubs.

Analostan Boat House, foot of New Hampshire avenue and F street.

Capitol Rowing Club, 602 F street n.w.

Columbia, foot of 32d street n.w.

Potomac, foot of 21st st. n.w.; meets 1st Monday in each month.

Washington Rowing Club, Cumberland's boat house, foot of 32d street n.w.

Washington Canoe Club, Cumberland's boat house, foot of 32d street n.w.

Clubs.

Barrett, 914 F street n.w. (Dramatic).

Capitol Bicycle, 413 15th street n.w.

Columbian, meets 1st Tuesday in each month at Pennsylvania avenue and 9th street n.w.

Cosmos, meets 1st Monday in every month, except July, Aug., and Sept., 23 Madison place n. w.

District Wheelmen, 905 M street n.w.

League of American Wheelmen, District of Columbia division; office of Secretary, corner of 15th and Pennsylvania avenue n.w.

Metropolitan, 1700 H street n.w.

Washington Cycle Club house, 1023 12th street n.w.

Woodmont Rod and Gun Club; B. E. J. Eils, Secretary and Treasurer, 707 7th street n.w.; club house and grounds in Washington County, Maryland.

Charitable and Benevolent.

American Association of the Red Cross, for the relief of suffering by war, pestilence, famine, flood, fires, and other calamities of sufficient magnitude to be deemed national in extent. President, Clara Barton; General Secretary, Clara Barton.

American Colonization Society, 450 Pennsylvania avenue n.w.; President, Hon. John H. B. Latrobe; Secretary and Treasurer, William Coppinger.

Associated Charities of the District of Columbia; President, President of Board of Commissioners of the D. C.; General Secretary, L. S. Emery. Office: 707 G street n.w.; open daily (except Sunday) from 10 a. m. to 5 p. m.

The Charity Organization Society of the District of Columbia, central office, room 11, 306 9th street n.w.; President, A. S. Pratt; Vice-Presidents, B. Pickman Mann, Mrs. S. A. Spencer.

Bakers' Benevolent Association; President, Hugo Schultz; Vice-President, L. Doerr; Recording Secretary, Paul Burk. Meets monthly at 606 11th street n.w.

Bakers' Union Beneficial Association, meets 2d Sunday at 609 C street n.w

Butchers' Beneficial Association, meets 1st Sunday of the month at 8th street, corner E n.w.

Capital Beneficial Association, meets 2d Sunday afternoon at 609 C street n.w.

Franklin Mutual Relief Association, meets 2d Monday, monthly, at St. Joseph's Hall, 5th street, corner H n.w.

German Benevolent Society; President, A. Romy; Secretary, Peter A. Mattern; meets at German Hall, 604 11th street n.w., 1st Monday in each month.

German Evangelical Beneficial Association; President, William Kettler; Secretary, William Scherger; meets at German Hall, 606 11th street n.w., 2d Tuesday in each month.

Gruetli Verein (Swiss Association); meets at St. George's Hall, 1st Thursday of each month; President, Henry Pfister; Recording Secretary, Chas. Gottenkieny.

Hebrew Fuel Society; President, Louis Rosenberg; Treasurer, Henry Franc.

Italian Benevolent Society; President, Domenico Christofani; Recording Secretary, C. P. Rallo; meets 2d Sunday in the month at Cosmopolitan Hall, 8th street, corner E n.w.

Ladies' (Lutheran) Church Society for the relief of the poor; President, Mr. Bartels; Secretary, Mrs. Fries; meets at German Hall, 606 11th street n.w., 2d Wednesday in each month.

Pensoara Free Kindergarten, 716 K streets n.w.; Mrs. Louisa Pollock, principal; Miss Annie Sutton, teacher.

Societe Francaise de Bienfaisance; President, Marquis de Chambrun; Corresponding Secretary, Mme. E. Sheridan; meets 2d Monday in each month at 723 14th street n.w.

Society for the Prevention of Cruelty to Animals; headquarters 1410 New York avenue n.w., President, Hon. Arthur MacArthur, 1201 N street n.w.; Agent, M. P. Key; meets on the 2d Tuesday of January in each year.

Phœnix Arbeiter Untersteutzungs Verein, meets every 1st and 3d Wednesday in the month at Red Men's Hall, 609 C street n.w.; Secretary, William Martin, 1628 5th street n.w.

Union Fraternelle de Langue Francaise, de Washington, D. C., meets at St. George's Hall, 510 11th street n.w., 1st Monday in every month; President, A. Laignel; Secretary, F. Moreau.

South Washington Beneficial Endowment Association, meets at corner 8th and C streets s.w. 1st Tuesday in each month; Secretary, E. J. Burtt.

Swiss Benevolent Association, Washington, D. C.; Secretary, August Tanner.

Verein Bayern; Secretary, Jacob Stinzing; meets 2d Sunday in each month in Cosmopolitan Hall.

Washington Sick Relief Association, meets 1st and 3d Mondays at 609 C street n.w.

Washington Deutcher Unterstutzungs Verein, meets at 1400 North Capitol street every 3d Thursday in each month; Secretary, Chas. F. Koxel.

Washington Butchers' Benevolent Association, meets at Cosmopolitan Hall the 1st Sunday in each month; Secretary, John Brown.

World's Peace Society and Arbitration League, 207 4½ street n.w., meets 1st Tuesday of each month; Corresponding Secretary, Dr. Robert McMurdy.

DENTAL.

The National Dental Association of the United States, meets in Washington biennially; Secretary, Dr. R. Finley Hunt, Washington, D. C.

Washington City Dental Society, 1113 Pennsylvania avenue n.w; Recording Secretary, G. L. Hills.

LEGAL.

Bar Association, meets 2d Tuesday in January, March, June, and October; Secretary, Leigh Robinson.

Patent Office Bar Association, meets at 633 F street n.w. 2d Monday in each month; Secretary and Acting Treasurer, Geo. S. Prindle.

LITERARY.

The Literary Society, meets every other Saturday evening, except during the summer, at house of some one of its members; Secretary, George Kennan.

The Jefferson Literary Society, meets every Monday evening in the Jefferson School Building, 6th street, corner D s.w. Literary exercises and debate; Secretary, William A. Johnson.

Unity Club, meets at members' houses, semi-monthly, on Friday evening; Secretary, Dexter A. Smith.

Carroll Institute, 602 F street n.w. Free reading room open every night, and free musical and literary entertainments every Thursday at 8 p. m., Corresponding Secretary, John Bingham.

The Literary and Debating Society of the National University, Law Department, meets every Thursday evening, except during the summer, at 1006 E street n.w.; President, E. N. Meekins; Secretary, A. J. Green.

The Argo Literary Society, meets every Sunday afternoon at Moore's Hall, 309 9th n.w.

The Moral Education Society of Washington, meets 3d Wednesday in each month at 2 o'clock p. m. at 1308 I n.w.; Corresponding Secretary, Dr. C. B. Winslow.

Concordia Reading Association, meets every evening at 707 I street n.w; Secretary, Adolph Adler.

The New England Society, 1309 Corcoran street; annual meetings Forefathers' day, December 20th each year; Secretary, Silas Boyce.

Georgetown University Alumni; Secretary, E. D. F. Brady.

Travel Club, social and literary, 810 12th street n.w.; Secretary, Miss Emily Brigham.

Washington Literary Association, meets every Sunday at 2 p. m. at German Hall, 606 11th street; President, Meyer Cohen.

Washington Lyceum Bureau, 529 7th street n.w.; Manager, George J. Presbrey.

Washington Free Kindergarten Building Association, 929 8th street n.w.; Corresponding Secretary, Mrs. E. B. Rankin.

Nursery-maids' Kindergarten Training School, Wednesdays, 3 to 4 p. m., 716 K n.w.

MEDICAL.

Medical Association of the District of Columbia, founded, 1833; Secretary, Lachlan Tyler.

Medical Society of the District of Columbia, meets every Wednesday at 8 o'clock p. m., at Georgetown University Law Building; Corresponding Secretary, T. C. Smith.

Medico-Chirurgical Society of District of Columbia, meets on the 1st and 3d Mondays of each month at 1321 F street n.w.; Secretary, L. A. Harvey.

Washington Homœopathic Medical Society; Secretary, Daniel H. Riggs.

MUSICAL.

Germania Maennerchor, meets at 8th, corner E st. n.w., every Thursday and Sunday evenings; Secretary, J. Charles Devantier.

Washington Musical Assembly, organized October 1st, 1885; meets at Elks' Hall, 902 Penna. avenue n.w.; R. F. Cardella, Secretary.

Washington Saengerbund, meets at 708 K street n.w., every Tuesday and Friday night at 8.30 p. m.; Recording Secretary, H. Meier.

RELIGIOUS.

Convent of Visitation, 1500 35th street n.w.

Notre Dame, K and North Capitol street n.e.

The Washington City Bible Society, organized in 1828; President, Rev. A. W. Pitzer; Secretary, J. V. A. Shields.

Women's Christian Association, 1719 13th street n.w; President, Mrs. Justice Strong; Secretary, Mrs. C. A. Weed, 1412 I street n.w.

Young Men's Christian Association, organized June 16, 1852; 1409 and 1411 New York avenue; open daily from 9 a. m. to 10 p. m.; General Secretary, T. A. Harding.

The Sunday School Union of the District of Columbia meets on the 4th Monday of every month in the lecture room of the Y. M. C. A. building; Secretary, Henry K. Simpson.

SCIENTIFIC.

Anthropological Society, meets every 1st and 2d Tuesday of each month from November to May, inclusive, at Columbia University building, corner H and 15th streets n.w.; President, Maj. J. W. Powell.

The Biological Society of Washington, meets alternate Saturdays, beginning October 31st, 1885, in the lecture room, National Museum; Secretaries, Richard Rathbun and Frank Baker.

Chemical Society of Washington; Secretary, A. C. Peale; meets monthly in Chemical lecture room of Columbian University, cor. 15th and H streets n.w.

Microscopical Society of Washington; Secretary, Edward M. Schaeffer, M. D.; meets at 1321 F street n.w., on 2d and 4th Tuesdays of each month.

The Philosophical Society of Washington, meets alternate Saturday evenings in the library of the Army Medical Museum; Secs., H. Farquhar and G. K. Gilbert.

TRADES.

National Federation of Labor Unions; President, E. W. Oyster.

Columbia Typographical Union No. 101, meets at St. Joseph's Hall every third Saturday; Secretary, Lloyd Prather.

District Photographic Association; Secretary, Clarence Dodge.

Washington Plate Printers' Society, meets 2d Monday in each month at German Hall.

Grocery Clerks' Association, meets at Shea's Hall 2d and 4th Tuesdays in each month.

Bricklayers' Union, meets 1st and 3d Friday evenings at Cosmopolitan Hall.

Carpenters' Union, meets Wednesday evenings at 13½ and E streets n.w.

Cigar Makers' Union, meets 2d and last Saturdays in each month at corner 4½ and Pennsylvania avenue n.w.

Granite Cutters' Union, meets 3d Thursday evenings at Red Men's Hall, 609 C street n.w.

Harness Makers' Union, meets Monday evenings at 709 G street n.w.

Journeymen Bookbinders' Society, meets 1st Tuesday evenings at Cooperative Hall, 1023 7th street n.w.

Journeymen Horseshoers' Union, meets 2d and 4th Tuesday evenings at Cosmopolitan Hall, 8th and E streets n.w.

Paper Hangers' Union meets every Thursday evening at Moore's Hall, 300 9th street n.w.

Pressmen's Union No. 1, meets 3d Saturday evenings at 8 o'clock at Knights of Labor's Hall, corner 4½ and Pennsylvania avenue n.w.

Stonemasons' Union, meets 2d Thursday evenings at St. George's Hall, 11th street n.w.

District Assembly Knights of Labor, meets 2d Sunday at Odeon Hall, corner 4½ and Pennsylvania avenue n.w.

Brickmakers' Assembly Knights of Labor No. 2448, meets Tuesday evenings at Odeon Hall.

Iron and Brass Workers' Assembly Knights of Labor No. 2905, meets Wednesday evenings at Shea's Hall, Pennsylvania ave n.w.

Journeymen Stone-Cutters' Assembly Knights of Labor No. 2563 meets 1st and 3d Friday evenings at Odeon Hall n.w.

Mixed Assembly Knights of Labor No. 2672, meets Thursday evenings at Odeon Hall, corner 4½ and Pennsylvania avenue n.w.

Painters' Assembly Knights of Labor No. 1798, meets Friday evenings at Shea's Hall.

Plasterers' Assembly Knights of Labor No. 1644, meets Monday evenings at Odeon Hall.

Plumbers' Assembly Knights of Labor No 2079 meets 1st and 3d Wednesday evenings at Odeon Hall.

Tailors' Assembly Knights of Labor No. 2370, meets 1st and 3d Saturday evenings at corner 4½ and Pennsylvania avenue n.w.

Tinners' Assembly Knights of Labor No. 2021 meets 2d and 3d evenings at Odeon Hall.

Stone-Rubbers' Assembly Knights of Labor, meets 1st and 3d Sundays at corner 4½ and Pennsylvania avenue n.w.

Coachmakers' Assembly Knights of Labor, meets 2d and 4th Fridays at corner of 4½ and Pennsylvania avenue n.w.

Confederation of Labor, meets every Tuesday at corner Pennsylvania avenue n.w.

Bookbinders' and Pressmen's Assembly Knights of Labor, every Thursday, corner 4½ and Pennsylvania avenue n.w.

Cigar Makers' Assembly Knights of Labor meets 2d and 4th Wednesdays at 609 C street n.w.

Mixed Assembly Knights of Labor, meets at 609 C street n.w.

CATHOLIC BENEVOLENT SOCIETIES.

Society of St. Vincent de Paul; Spiritual Director, Rev. J. A. Walter; Council meets on the 1st Wednesday of every month, at the residence of the Spiritual Director.

Catholic Knights of America.

St. Aloysius Branch No. 170; Secretary, W. F. Clarkson.
St. Peter's Branch No. 199; Secretary, Joseph Waltemeyer.
St. Dominic Branch No. 212; Secretary, John J. Dermody.
Carroll Branch No. 224; Secretary, Frank N. Devereaux.

Miscellaneous.

Young Catholics' Friends Society. The general society meets quarterly and the parochial divisions monthly. The object is the education of poor children; Secretary, M. B. Saxton.

Young Catholics' Friends Society, Georgetown; Secretary, T. F. S. King; meets 1st Monday in each month, at School Hall, Georgetown.

St. Patrick's Division; Secretary, C. L. Clarke.
St. Peter's Division; Secretary, John Mawdsley.
St. Dominic's Division; Secretary, J. J. Dermody.
St. Aloysius' Division; Secretary, John J. Fuller.
St. Mary's Division; Secretary, J. H. Schultheis.

Immaculate Conception Division; Secretary, Patrick Vaughan; meets 1st Sunday of each month after high mass at Church Hall, N street, near 8th n.w.

St. John's Association meets 2d Monday of each month in Church Hall, N street, near 8th n.w.

St. Joseph's Benevolent Association meets 2d Tuesdays at St. Joseph's Hall.

Washington Hibernian Society meets 1st and 2d Thursdays in each month.

Washington Hibernian Society No. 3, Capitol Hill, meets monthly at Washington Hall.

Georgetown Hibernian Benevolent Society meets monthly at 3d street, corner Prospect avenue.

Knights of St. Bernard meet monthly in Trinity Parish (Catholic) School-house, 36th street, corner N n.w.

Knights of St. Columbkill, St. Aloysius Parish, meet monthly.

Knights of St. George No. 1 meet 1st Monday, monthly, at St. Joseph's Hall.

Knights of St. Joseph of Immaculate Conception Parish meet monthly in parish school-house.

Knights of St. Patrick meet at Cosmopolitan Hall, on the 1st and 3d Monday in every month and every Sunday afternoon.

Junior Knights of St. Patrick meet at G street, corner N. J. avenue n.w.

Knights of St. Peter meet 1st Monday in the month in basement of St. Peter's Church.

Knights of St. Stephen meet 1st Thursday in each month, 19th street and Pennsylvania avenue n.w.

Knights of St. Augustine No. 2 meet monthly at 1218 E n.w.

St. Boniface Beneficial Association meets 2d Wednesday of every month at St. Joseph's Hall, 5th and H streets n.w.

Georgetown Catholic Benevolent Total Abstinence Society meets Sunday evening at Society Hall, Georgetown.

CEMETERIES.

Baptist, near Drovers' Rest.
Battle Ground Cemetery, 7th-street road, near Brightwood
Belt's family, north of Tennallytown.
Berry, family, Hillsdale.
Brightwood Cemetery, Brightwood.
Cephas, family, Conduit road, near Drovers' Rest.
Chappell's, private, northeast of Tennallytown.
Christian, Chappell farm, near Tennallytown.
College, private, Georgetown.
Columbian Harmony Burial Ground, colored, Brentwood.
Congressional Burial Ground, on eastern branch of the Potomac.
Convent of Visitation, private, 35th and P streets n.w
Dangerfield, family.
Dean's, private, Sheriff road.
Garden's, private, near Anacostia road.
Glenwood Cemetery, Lincoln avenue.
Good Hope, Hamilton road.
Graceland Cemetery, terminus of H street n.e.
Green Vale, near Tennallytown.
Harmonia, Brentwood road.
Hebbons', family, Broad-branch road.
Hillsdale Cemetery, Hillsdale.
Holyrood Cemetery, High and Fayette streets, Georgetown.
Howard's private, Anacostia road.
Insane Asylum.
Jenkins' private, Jenkins' farm.
Jew's Burial Ground, Adas Israel and Washington Hebrew, one mile from Government Insane Asylum.
Jones' Chapel, Bennings' Station.
McPherson's private, Hillsdale.
Macedonia, near Sheridan avenue, Hillsdale.
Macpelah, Hamilton road.
Methodist, Tennallytown.
Methodist Burial Ground, opposite Congressional burial.

Moore's, Hillsdale.
Mount Olivet Cemetery, Catholic, Bladensburg road.
Mount Pleasant Plain Cemetery, young men's burial ground, colored, one mile northwest of Columbia College.
Mount Zion, Mill street, between P and Q n.w.
Oak Hill Cemetery, head of 30th street n.w.
Payne's, Bennings Station.
Potter's Field, Washington Asylum.
Presbyterian Cemetery, 34th street above Q n.w.
Prospect Hill Cemetery, German Lutheran, Lincoln avenue.
Rock Creek Cemetery, near Soldiers' Home.
St. Mary's German Catholic, Lincoln avenue.
St. Patrick's, Catholic, Boundary near 3d street, n.w.
Scaggs', Anacostia road.
Shoemaker's Farm, near Pierce's Mills.
Shoemaker, family, near Tennallytown.
Smith's, Hamilton road.
Soldiers' Home National Cemetery, Harewood road.
Swartz, private, near Brightwood.

CONGRESS.

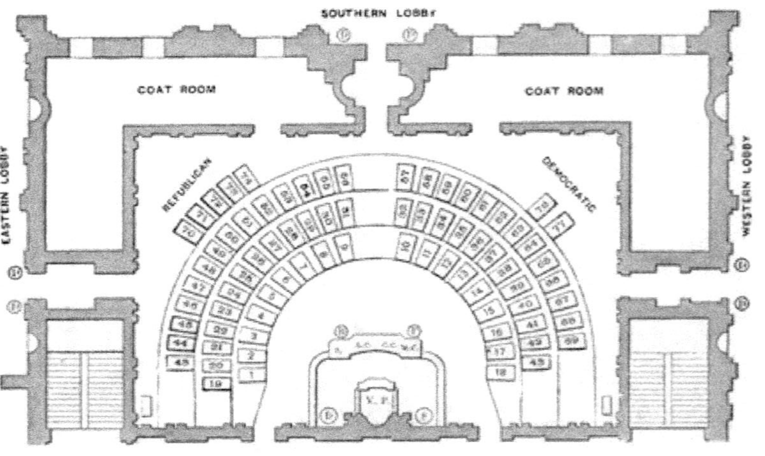
SOUTHERN LOBBY
COAT ROOM
COAT ROOM
EASTERN LOBBY
WESTERN LOBBY
REPUBLICAN
DEMOCRATIC
V. P.

SENATORS OF THE UNITED STATES,

FORTY-NINTH CONGRESS.

For biographies of Senators and Representatives, full lists of Committees, etc., see Ben: Perley Poor's Congressional Directory.

No. Seat.

11. Morgan, J T, Selma, Alabama.
68. Pugh, J L, Eufaula, "

18. Berry, J H, Washington, Ark.
17. Jones, J K, Bentonville, "

68. Hearst, Geo, San Francisco, Cal.
43. Stanford, Leland, " "

71. Bowen, T M, Del Norte, Colorado.
46. Teller, H M, Central City, "

2. Hawley, J R, Hartford, Conn.
3. Platt, O H, Meriden, "

41. Gray, G, New Castle, Delaware.
65. Saulsbury, E, Dover, "

39. Call, W, Jacksonville, Florida.
33. Jones, C W, Pensacola, "

10. Brown, J E, Atlanta, Georgia.
16. Colquitt, A H, " "

47. Cullom, S M, Springfield, Illinois.
8. Logan, J A, Chicago, "

25. Harrison, Benj, Indianapolis, Ind.
36. Voorhees, D W, Terre Haute, "

30. Allison, W B, Dubuque, Iowa.
1. Wilson, J F, Fairfield, "

29. Ingalls, J J, Atchison, Kansas.
26. Plumb, P B, Emporia, "

37. Beck, J B, Lexington, Kentucky.
40. Blackburn, J C S, Versailles, "

60. Eustis, J B, New Orleans, La.
50. Gibson, R L, " "

5. Frye, W P, Lewiston, Maine.
24. Hale, E, Ellsworth, "

35. Gorman, A P, Laurel, Maryland.
42. Wilson, E K, Snow Hill, "

31. Dawes, Henry L, Pittsfield, Mass.
27. Hoar, G F, Worcester, "

48. Conger, O D, Port Huron, Mich.
23. Palmer, T W, Detroit, "

51. McMillan, S J R, St. Paul, Minn.
20. Sabin, D M, Stillwater, "

No. Seat.

38. George, J Z, Jackson, Mississippi.
67. Walthall, E C, Grenada, "

13. Cockrell, F M, Warrensburg, Mo.
34. Vest, G G, Kansas City, "

73. Manderson, Chas F, Omaha, Neb.
55. Van Wyck, C H, Nebraska City, "

57. Fair, J G, Virginia City, Nevada.
59. Jones, J P, Gold Hill, "

19. Blair, H W, Manchester, N. H.
72. Pike, A P, Franklin, "

61. McPherson, J R, Jersey City, N. J.
54. Sewell, W J, Camden, "

44. Evarts, W M, New York, N. Y.
28. Miller, W, Herkimer, "

32. Ransom, M W, Weldon, N. C.
64. Vance, Z B, Charlotte, "

58. Payne, Henry B, Cleveland, Ohio.
26. Sherman, John, Mansfield, "

22. Dolph, J N, Portland, Oregon.
75. Mitchell, J H, " "

4. Cameron, J D, Harrisburg, Pa.
45. Mitchell, J I, Wellsboro', "

52. Aldrich, N W, Providence, R. I.
45. Chace, J, "

12. Butler, M C, Edgefield, S. C.
77. Hampton, W, Charleston, "

15. Harris, Isham G, Memphis, Tenn.
69. Whitthorne, W C, Columbia, "

14. Coke, R, Waco, Texas.
16. Maxey, S B, Paris, "

7. Edmunds, G F, Burlington, Vt.
5. Morrill, J S, Strafford, "

6. Mahone, W, Petersburg, Virginia.
53. Riddleberger, H H, Woodstock, "

62. Camden, J N, Parkersburg, W. Va.
63. Kenna, J E, Charleston, "

82. Sawyer, P, Oshkosh, Wisconsin.
76. Spooner, J C, Hudson, "

President *pro tempore*—John Sherman, 1319 K street nw.

Secretary of the Senate—Anson G. McCook, Arlington Hotel.

Sergeant-at-Arms of the Senate—William P. Canady, 302 Delaware ave. ne.

Chaplain to the Senate—Rev. E. D. Huntley, D. D., 1329 K street nw.

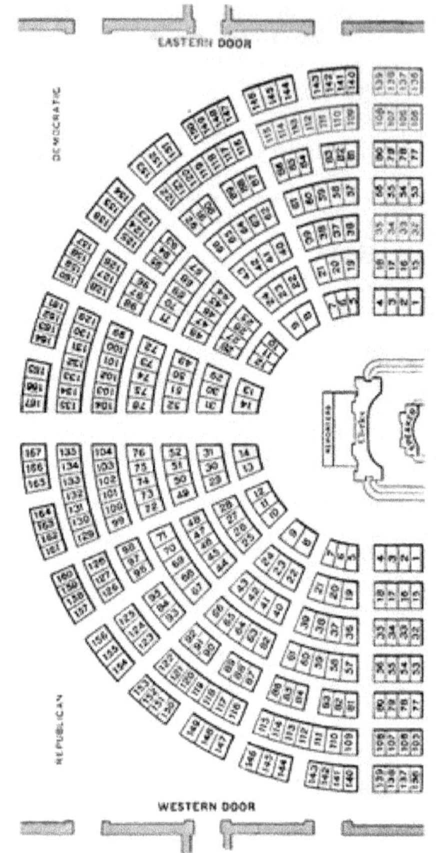
EASTERN DOOR
DEMOCRATIC
REPUBLICAN
WESTERN DOOR

MEMBERS OF THE HOUSE OF REPRESENTATIVES

FORTY-NINTH CONGRESS.

"R" and "L" signifies Right (Democratic) and Left (Republican) side of the Speaker's chair.

Alabama.

No.	Seat.		Dist.
75	R	Jas T Jones, Demopolis	1
131	R	H A Herbert, Montgomery	2
28	R	Wm C Oates, Abbeville	3
148	R	A C Davidson, Uniontown	4
130	R	Thos W Sadler, Prattville	5
79	L	John M Martin, Tuscaloosa	6
62	R	Wm H Forney, Jacksonville	7
113	R	Joseph Wheeler, Wheeler	8

Arkansas.

No.	Seat.		Dist.
2	R	P Dunn, Forest City	1
68	R	C R Breckinridge, Pine Bluff	2
67	R	Thos C McRae, Prescott	3
45	R	John H Rodgers, Fort Smith	4
8	R	Sam'l W Peel, Bentonville	5

California.

No.	Seat.		Dist.
47	R	Barclay Henley, Santa Rosa	1
110	L	J A Louttit, Stockton	2
83	L	Joseph McKenna, Suisun	3
42	L	W W Morrow, San Francisco	4
22	L	Chas N Felton, San Mateo	5
100	L	H H Markham, Los Angeles	6

Colorado.

No.	Seat.		Dist.
74	L	George G Symes, Denver	1

Connecticut.

No.	Seat.		Dist.
70	L	John R Buck, Hartford	1
143	L	C L Mitchell, New Haven	2
139	L	John T Wait, Norwich	3
118	R	E W Seymour, Litchfield	4

Delaware.

No.	Seat.		Dist.
77	R	Chas B Lore, Wilmington	1

Florida.

No.	Seat.		Dist.
164	R	R H M Davidson, Quincy	1
160	R	C Dougherty, Port Orange	2

Georgia.

No.	Seat.		Dist.
98	R	Thos M Norwood, Savannah	1
134	R	Henry G Turner, Quitman	2
13	R	Charles F Crisp, Americus	3
87	R	Henry R Harris, Greenville	4
46	R	N J Hammond, Atlanta	5
97	R	James H Blount, Macon	6

Georgia—Cont'd.

No.	Seat.		Dist.
38	R	J C Clements, La Fayette	7
119	R	Seaborn Reese, Sparta	8
117	R	Allen D Candler, Gainesville	9
116	R	George T Barnes, Augusta	10

Illinois.

No.	Seat.		Dist.
157	L	R W Dunham, Chicago	1
6	R	Frank Lawler, Chicago	2
72	R	James H Ward, Chicago	3
101	L	George E Adams, Chicago	4
151	L	A J Hopkins, Aurora	5
136	L	Robert R Hitt, Mt Morris	6
71	L	T J Henderson, Princeton	7
24	L	Ralph Plumb, Streator	8
21	L	Lewis E Payson, Pontiac	9
57	R	N E Worthington, Peoria	10
137	R	William H Neece, Macomb	11
76	R	James M Riggs, Winchester	12
92	R	W M Springer, Springfield	13
94	L	J H Rowell, Bloomington	14
69	L	Joseph G Cannon, Danville	15
108	L	S Z Landes, Mount Carmel	16
10	R	John R Eden, Sullivan	17
43	R	Wm R Morrison, Waterloo	18
162	L	R W Townshend, Shawneetown	19
41	L	John R Thomas, Metropolis	20

Indiana.

No.	Seat.		Dist.
139	R	John J Kleiner, Evansville	1
56	R	Thomas R Cobb, Vincennes	2
165	R	J G Howard, Jeffersonville	3
24	R	William S Holman, Aurora	4
142	R	C C Matson, Greencastle	5
87	L	T M Browne, Winchester	6
82	L	W D Bynum, Indianapolis	7
65	L	Jas T Johnston, Rockville	8
64	R	Thos B Ward, La Fayette	9
43	L	Wm D Owen, Logansport	10
51	L	George W Steele, Marion	11
158	R	Robert Lowry, Fort Wayne	12
120	R	George Ford, South Bend	13

Iowa.

No.	Seat.		Dist.
121	R	B J Hall, Burlington	1
133	R	J H Murphy, Davenport	2
132	L	D B Henderson, Dubuque	3
163	L	Wm E Fuller, West Union	4
152	R	B T Frederick, Marshallt'wn	5
31	R	J B Weaver, Bloomfield	6
46	L	Edwin H Conger, Adel	7

Iowa—Cont'd.

No. Seat. Dist.

153 L...Wm P Hepburn, Clarinda... 8
124 L...Jos Lyman, Council Bluffs... 9
52 L...Adoniram J Holmes, Boone...10
76 L...Isaac S Struble, Le Mars...11

Kansas.

119 L...E N Morrill, Hiawatha... 1
165 L...E H Funston, Iola... 2
161 L...Bishop W Perkins, Oswego... 3
150 L...Thomas Ryan, Topeka... 4
1 L...J A Anderson, Manhattan... 5
112 L...L Hanback, Osborne City... 6
163 L...Sam'l R Peters, Newton... 7

Kentucky.

23 R...Wm J Stone, Eddyville... 1
25 R...Polk Laffoon, Madisonville... 2
131 R...J E Halsell, Bowling Green... 3
140 R...T A Robertson, Hodgenville 4
122 R...Albert S Willis, Louisville... 5
Speaker...J G Carlisle, Covington... 6
69 R...W C P Breckinridge, Lexington... 7
141 R...Jas B McCreary, Richmond. 8
72 L...W H Wadsworth, Maysville. 9
7 R...W P Taulbee, Salyersville...10
18 R...Frank L Wolford, Columbia 11

Louisiana.

166 R...L St Martin, New Orleans... 1
127 R...Nath'l D Wallace, " ... 2
98 R...Edw J Gay, Plaquemine... 3
85 R...N C Blanchard, Shreveport... 4
78 R...J Floyd King, Vidalia... 5
135 R...Alfred B Irion, Marksville... 6

Maine.

129 L...Thomas B Reed, Portland... 1
26 L...N Dingley, Jr, Lewiston... 2
126 L...Seth L Milliken, Belfast... 3
177 L...Charles A Boutelle, Bangor... 4

Maryland.

42 R...Charles H Gibson, Easton... 1
68 R...Frank T Shaw, Westminster. 2
59 R...——, Baltimore... 3
29 R...J V L Findlay, Baltimore... 4
159 R...Barnes Compton, Annapolis 5
125 L...L E McComas, Hagerstown... 6

Massachusetts.

66 L...Robt T Davis, Fall River... 1
3 L...John D Long, Hingham... 2
136 L...Ambrose A Ranney, Boston. 3
35 R...Patrick A Collins, Boston... 4
28 L...Edw D Hayden, Woburn... 5
5 R...Henry B Lovering, Lynn... 6
49 L...Eben F Stone, Newburyport 7
37 L...Charles H Allen, Lowell... 8
50 L...Fred'k D Ely, Dedham... 9

Massachusetts—Cont'd.

No. Seat. Dist.

58 L...William W Rice, Worcester.10
36 L...William Whiting, Holyoke...11
162 L...F W Rockwell, Pittsfield...12

Michigan.

49 R...William C Maybury, Detroit 1
86 R...Nath'l B Eldredge, Adrian... 2
64 L...James O'Donnell, Jackson... 3
128 L...J C Burrows, Kalamazoo... 4
40 R...C C Comstock, Grand Rapids 5
33 R...Edward B Winans, Hamburg 6
145 R...E C Carleton, Port Huron... 7
147 R...T E Tarsney, East Saginaw. 8
4 L...B M Cutcheon, Manistee... 9
112 R...S O Fisher, West Bay City...10
96 L...S C Moffatt, Traverse City...11

Minnesota.

115 L...Milo White, Chatfield... 1
81 L...J B Wakefield, Blue Earth City... 2
95 L...H B Strait, Shakopee... 3
8 L...J B Gilfillan, Minneapolis... 4
7 L...Knute Nelson, Alexandria... 5

Mississippi.

106 R...John M Allen, Tupelo... 1
108 R...J B Morgan, Hernando... 2
163 R...T C Catchings, Vicksburg... 3
139 L...F G Barry, West Point... 4
63 R...O R Singleton, Forest... 5
108 R...H S Van Eaton, Woodville... 6
76 R...E Barksdale, Jackson... 7

Missouri.

95 R...William H Hatch, Hannibal 1
101 R...John B Hale, Carrollton... 2
27 R...Alex M Dockery, Gallatin... 3
123 R...James N Burnes, St Joseph.. 4
98 L...Wm Warner, Kansas City... 5
126 R...John T Heard, Sedalia... 6
91 R...John E Hutton, Mexico... 7
153 R...John J O'Neill, St Louis... 8
1 R...John M Glover, " ... 9
111 R...M L Clardy, Farmington...10
73 R...Rich'd P Bland, Lebanon...11
51 L...William J Stone, Nevada...12
97 L...Wm H Wade, Springfield...13
141 L...Wm Dawson, New Madrid...14

Nebraska.

35 L...A J Weaver, Falls City... 1
39 L...James Laird, Hastings... 2
122 L...Geo W E Dorsey, Fremont... 3

Nevada.

18 L...W Woodburn, Virginia City. 1

New Hampshire.

155 L...M A Haynes, Lake Village... 1
102 L...J H Gallinger, Concord... 2

New Jersey.

No. Seat. Dist.
143 L...George Hires, Salem ... 1
22 L...James Buchanan, Trenton... 2
55 R...Rufus S Green, Elizabeth ... 3
15 R...J N Pidcock, White House Station ... 4
54 L...Wm W Phelps, Englewood.. 5
146 L...Herman Lehlbach, Newark.. 6
19 R...Wm McAdoo, Jersey City.... 7

New York.

4 R...Perry Belmont, Babylon ... 1
154 R...Felix Campbell, Brooklyn... 2
11 L...Darwin R James, " ... 3
128 R...Peter P Mahoney, " ... 4
93 R...Archibald M Bliss, " ... 5
100 R...Nicholas Muller, New York.. 6
58 R...John J Adams, " ... 7
14 R...T J Campbell, " ... 8
9
70 R...Abram S Hewitt, " ...10
157 R...T A Merriman, " ...11
65 L...Abraham Dowdney, " ...12
54 R...Egbert L Viele, " ...13
44 R...W G Stahlnecker, Yonkers..14
14 R...Lewis Beach, Cornwall ...15
56 L...J H Ketcham, Dover Plains.16
183 L...James G Lindsley, Rondout.17
156 L...H G Burleigh, Whitehall ...18
17 L...John Swinburne, Albany ...19
12 L...George West, Ballston...20
57 L...F A Johnson, Glens Falls ...21
45 L...Abrah'm X Parker, Potsdam.22
33 R...J Thomas Spriggs, Utica...23
106 R...John S Pindar, Cobleskill...24
138 L...Frank Hiscock, Syracuse. ...25
131 L...S C Millard, Binghamton...26
131 L...Sereno E Payne, Auburn...27
36 R...John Arnot, Elmira...28
84 L...Ira Davenport, Bath...29
112 L...Charles S Baker, Rochester.30
164 L...John G Sawyer, Albion ...31
152 L...John M Farquhar, Buffalo...32
111 L...J B Weber, West Seneca...33
150 L...W L Sessions, Jamestown...34

North Carolina.

107 L...Thos G Skinner, Hertford... 1
86 L...James E O'Hara, Enfield... 2
119 R...W J Green, Fayetteville... 3
125 R...William R Cox, Raleigh... 4
96 R...James W Reid, Wentworth... 5
80 R...R T Bennett, Wadesborough. 6
79 R...J S Henderson, Salisbury.... 7
125 R...W H H Cowles, Wilkesborough ... 8
60 R...Thos D Johnston, Asheville. 9

Ohio.

164 L...B Butterworth, Cincinnati... 1
130 L...Chas E Brown, " ... 2
77 L...Jas E Campbell, Hamilton... 3
39 R...C M Anderson, Greenville ... 4
9 R...Benj Le Fevre, Maplewood.. 5

Ohio—Cont'd.

No. Seat. Dist.
124 R...William D Hill, Defiance... 6
66 R...George E Seney, Tiffin... 7
19 L...John Little, Xenia... 8
89 L...Wm C Cooper, Mt Vernon... 9
143 L...Jacob Romeis, Toledo...10
156 R...W W Ellsberry, Georgetown.11
90 L...A C Thompson, Portsmouth.12
34 L...Jos H Outhwaite, Columbus.13
63 L...Chas H Grosvenor, Athens...14
3 R...Beriah Wilkins, Uhrichsville..15
126 L...Geo W Geddes, Mansfield...16
21 R...A J Warner, Marietta ...17
93 L...Isaac H Taylor, Carrollton...18
88 L...Ezra B Taylor, Warren...19
5 L...W McKinley, Jr., Canton...20
82 R...Martin A Foran, Cleveland...21

Oregon.

135 L...Binger Herman, Roseburg. 1

Pennsylvania.

28 L...Edwin S Osborne (At Large), Wilkesbarre.
24 L...H H Bingham, Philadelphia 1
116 L...Chas O'Neill, " ... 2
40 R...Sam'l J Randall, " ... 3
48 L...Wm D Kelley, " ... 4
10 L...Alfred C Harmer " ... 5
32 L...J B Everhart, West Chester 6
40 L...I N Evans, Hatborough ... 7
57 R...D Ermentrout, Reading ... 8
92 L...John A Hiestand, Lancaster 9
34 R...Wm H Sowden, Allentown...10
25 R...J B Storm, Stroudsburg...11
38 L...Jos A Scranton, Scranton...12
6 L...Chas N Brumm, Minersville.13
91 L...Franklin Bound, Milton...14
27 L...F C Bunnell, Tunkhannock.15
73 L...Wm W Brown, Bradford...16
80 L...J M Campbell, Johnstown...17
144 L...L E Atkinson, Mifflintown...18
61 R...John A Swope, Gettysburg...19
107 R...A G Curtin, Bellefonte...20
26 R...Chas E Boyle, Uniontown...21
9 L...Jas S Negley, Pittsburgh...22
90 L...Thomas M Bayne, Bellevue...23
41 L...O L Jackson, New Castle...24
167 L...A C White, Brookville ...25
60 L...George W Fleeger, Butler ...26
130 R...William L Scott, Erie...27

Rhode Island.

68 L...H J Spooner, Providence... 1
123 L...Wm A Pirce, Olneyville... 2

South Carolina.

72 R...Samuel Dibble, Orangeburg 1
100 R...G D Tillman, Edgefield... 2
72 R...D Wyatt Aiken, Cokesbury.. 3
99 R...Wm H Perry, Greenville... 4
65 R...John J Hemphill, Chester ... 5
74 R...Geo W Dargan, Darlington.. 6
118 L...Robert Smalls, Beaufort... 7

TENNESSEE.

No. Seat.		Dist.
39 L	A H Pettibone, Greenville	1
104 L	L C Houk, Knoxville	2
129 R	John R Neal, Rhea Springs	3
37 R	Benton McMillin, Carthage	4
105 R	J D Richardson, Murfreesboro	5
29 R	A J Caldwell, Nashville	6
12 R	J G Ballentine, Pulaski	7
59 R	John M Taylor, Lexington	8
18 R	P T Glass, Ripley	9
75 L	Zach Taylor, Covington	10

TEXAS.

No. Seat.		Dist.
53 R	Charles Stewart, Houston	1
102 R	J H Reagan, Palestine	2
141 R	J H Jones, Henderson	3
111 R	D B Culberson, Jefferson	4
71 R	J W Throckmorton, McKinney	5
17 R	Olin Wellborn, Dallas	6
101 R	W H Crain, Cuero	7
161 R	J F Miller, Gonzales	8
115 R	R Q Mills, Corsicana	9
19 R	J D Sayers, Bastrop	10
162 R	S W T Lanham, Weatherford	11

VERMONT.

No. Seat.		Dist.
151 L	J W Stewart, Middlebury	1
148 L	William W Grout, Barton	2

VIRGINIA.

No. Seat.		Dist.
11 R	T Croxton, Tappahannock	1
15 L	H Libbey, Old Point Comfort	2
41 R	George D Wise, Richmond	3
62 L	James D Brady, Petersburg	4
90 R	George C Cabell, Danville	5
107 R	J W Daniel, Lynchburg	6
130 R	C T O'Ferrall, Harrisonburg	7
33 L	J S Barbour, Alexandria	8
106 L	C F Trigg, Abingdon	9
135 R	J R Tucker, Lexington	10

WEST VIRGINIA.

No. Seat.		Dist.
67 L	Nathan Goff, Jr, Clarksburg	1
23 R	Wm L Wilson, Charlestown	2
123 R	Chas P Snyder, Charleston	3
132 R	Eustace Gibson, Huntington	4

WISCONSIN.

No. Seat.		Dist.
29 L	L B Caswell, Fort Atkinson	1
147 R	Edw S Bragg, Fond du Lac	2
106 L	R M La Follette, Madison	3
44 L	I W Van Schaick, Milwaukee	4
138 L	Thos R Hudd, Green Bay	5
59 L	Rich'd Guenther, Oshkosh	6
13 L	O B Thomas, Prairie du Chien	7
20 L	W T Price, Black River Falls	8
135 L	I Stephenson, Marinette	9

TERRITORIAL DELEGATES.

ARIZONA.

No. Seat.		
87 L	Curtis C Bean	Prescott

DAKOTA.

No. Seat.		
101 L	Oscar S Gifford	Canton

IDAHO.

No. Seat.		
140 L	John Hailey	Boise City

MONTANA.

No. Seat.		
83 R	Joseph K Toole	Helena

NEW MEXICO.

No. Seat.		
94 R	Antonio Joseph	Ojo Caliente

UTAH.

No. Seat.		
143 R	John T Caine	Salt Lake City

WASHINGTON.

No. Seat.		
109 L	Charles S Voorhees	Colfax

WYOMING.

No. Seat.		
95 L	Joseph M Carey	Cheyenne

Speaker—John G. Carlisle, Riggs House.

Clerk—John B. Clark, Jr., 2011 P street nw.

Sergeant-at-Arms—J. P. Leedom, 117 B street se.

Doorkeeper—Samuel Donelson, The Clarendon.

Postmaster—Lycurgus Dalton, 210 North Capitol street.

Chaplain—W. H. Milburn, D. D., New York avenue.

DIRECTORY OF BUSINESS HOUSES.

DIRECTORY

OF

PRINCIPAL BUSINESS HOUSES

OF

WASHINGTON, D. C.

REFERENCES.—The letters M. and T., with numbers below, which appear after the address of each firm, refer to the Margin and Tape on the Map accompanying this book. Thus, to find the location of the Arlington Publishing Co., which appears under the head of Art Publishers as M. 46, T. 45, we place the tape on 46 on the marginal scale of the Map and at 45 on the tape, is found the Corcoran Building, where their office is located.

For alphabetical lists of all the business houses in the city see Boyd's Directory, published annually in January.

	M.	T.
Abstract of Titles of City Property.		
Barnard M C, 472 La av nw	48	40
Lawyers' Title Co, 342 D nw	48	39
Patch John, 506 10th nw	47	43
Real Estate Title Insurance Co, D.C., The, 472 La av nw	48	40
Agents, Claim.		
Bancroft G & Co, 635 G nw	15	41
BEARD HENRY, 923 F nw (see page 153)	46	42
Lincoln W S, 630 9th nw	46	42
Richards, A C, 468 La av nw	48	40
Spalding H, 50 Corcoran bld	46	45
Wright J P & S J, 625 6th nw	46	40
Agents, Collecting.		
Lockett Samuel T, 1228 F nw	46	44
Merchants' Association, 529 7th nw	47	41
Stahl Thomas B, 452 D nw	47	39
Agents, General.		
Hogue John J, 3015 N nw	53	56
COOLIDGE GEO A, 29 Corcoran bldg (see page 226)	46	45
Kinsell Robert H, 530 9th nw	47	42
Agents, Insurance.		
(See Insurance Agents.)		
Agents, Land.		
Brackett Fred, 1108 F nw	46	45
Curtiss & Burdett, 925 F nw	46	42
Heaton Frank M, 517 F nw	46	42
Hill W C, 630 9th nw	46	42
Moulton C H, 928 F nw	46	42
Smith J Dempster, 1420 F nw	46	45

	M.	T.
Agents, Mercantile and Commercial.		
Bradstreet's, New Glenton bldg, 9th c Pa av nw	48	42
Dun R G & Co, 1403 Pa av nw	47	45
Agents, National Bank.		
Barnett Jos S, 138 Pa av se	53	34
Pratt A S & Son, 401 9th nw	47	42
Agents, News.		
National News Bureau, 530 9th	47	42
Union News Co, N J av c C	49	37
Agents, Patent.		
(See Patent Solicitors and Attorneys.)		
Cook Thomas & Son, 1331 Pa av nw	18	44
Reed Alvin L, 511 Pa av nw	50	44
Agents, Real Estate.		
(See Real Estate Agents and Brokers.)		
Agents, Steamship.		
Bell & Co, 1117 Pa av nw	47	45
Agricultural Implements.		
Baker J A, 928 La av nw	50	42
Cropley, Boteler & Crampton, 3260 M nw	18	54
Mann P, 307 7th sw	51	41
Aquaria.		
Schaffer S, 635 D nw	48	41

	M.	T.
Architects.		
Fleming R I, 1416 F nw	46	45
Fraser J, 1425 N Y av nw	44	45
Gray W B, 600 13th nw	44	46
Mullett A B, 1411 F nw	46	45
Poindexter W M, 703 15th nw	46	45
PAGE H L, 1515 H nw (see page 213)	43	45
SMITHMEYER J L & CO, 703 15th nw (see page 187)	44	45
Art Publishers.		
ARLINGTON PUBLISHING CO, 29 Corcoran building (see page 221)	46	45
Artists.		
FORSBERG G W, 80 Corcoran building	46	45
BOYLE A E, 945 Pa av nw (see page 600)	48	42
MORRELL J M, May build'g, cor 7th and E nw (see page 159)	46	41
SCHUTTER H, 727 9th nw (see page 288)	43	42
Weyl Max, 945 Pa av nw	48	42
Artists' Materials.		
(See Paints, Oils, &c.)		
Attorneys-at-Law.		
Appleby & Edmonston, 428 5th nw	47	40
Bigelow J G, 503½ D nw	48	40
BRITTON & GRAY, 622-626 F nw (see page 200)	46	41
Cressey C E, 32 Corcoran bldg	46	45
Ellis E J, 1416 F nw	46	45
HENDERSON W G, 925 9th nw (see page 163)	43	41
SPEAR ELLIS, 922 F nw (see page 193)	46	42
Lemon G E, 615 15th nw	44	45
Auctioneers.		
Dowling T, Pa av, cor 11th nw	49	43
Williams W B & Co, 1008 Pa av nw	49	42
Awning-Makers.		
Burton R C, 434 9th nw	47	42
Copeland M G & Co, 645 La av nw	50	41
Bakers.		
CHARLTON B & CO, 472-476 C nw (general—see page 204)	49	40
Crogan J G, 422 La av nw (crackers)	47	40
Kennedy F A Co, 430 11th nw (crackers—Cambridge, Mass.)	48	43
Krafft G S & Son, 1746 Pa av nw	42	48
Schneider Wm J, 230 E Cap	31	34
STOLPP C J, cor 6th and G nw	45	41
Vogt J L, 927 Pa av nw	49	42
Banks.		
(See page 75.)		
Bankers.		
Bateman & Co, 1411 F nw	44	45
Bell & Co, 1437 Pa av nw	42	45
Crane, Parris & Co, 1344 F nw	46	44
Corson & Macartney, 1419 F nw	44	45
Johnson Lewis & Co, Pa av cor 10th nw	49	52
Riggs & Co, Pa av cor 15th nw	44	45
Bankers and Brokers.		
MAYSE W & CO, 516 9th nw (see page 227)	46	42
Barbers.		
BURGESS H C, 8th and D nw (see page 165)	48	41
WATSON C J, 7th and D nw (see page 195)	48	41
WILSON J & M D, 704 E nw (see page 162)	47	41
Wilson H, Ebbitt House	46	44
Bell-Hangers.		
(See Locksmiths, &c.)		
Bicycles and Tricycles.		
Brenner E H, 1006 E nw	46	43
Christ & Higham, 905 G nw	44	42
Owen H S, 1400 N Y av nw	47	45
Smith, Bro & Co, 1206 Pa av nw	47	43
Baths.		
(See Barbers.)		
Bill Posters.		
Moxley Lloyd, 408 10th nw	43	45
Poole C W, 506 D nw	47	35
Billiard Saloons.		
Beck John, 631 La av nw	50	41
Miller & Jones, 1323 E nw	47	44
Scanlon Michael, 413 9th nw	48	42
Bleachers.		
Packer & Woolston, 302 E nw	47	41
Whiting A T, 924 Pa av nw	49	42
Boarding Houses.		
Bradley S T Mrs, 1402 N Y av nw	49	45
Crist M F, 424 6th nw	47	41
Gilliam E F, 939 H nw	43	42
Humphries E A Mrs, 906 14th nw	41	44
Kendall M C, 1324 Vt av nw	35	43
Olcott M L, 500 E nw	47	40
Phillips M E, 911 N Y av nw	42	42
Ricketts M J, 335 H nw	44	42
Boats and Boat Builders.		
CUMBERLAND J & SON, 27th near F nw (see p 184)	43	53
PASSENO J, 3124 Water st nw (see page 174)	9	56

	S.	T.
Books, Periodicals, and Stationery.		
Ballantyne Wm & Son 428 7th	47	43
Brentano Bros, 1015 Pa av nw	49	43
BRENNAN D A, 612 9th nw (Catholic—see page 169)	45	42
DECKER & CO, 1111 F nw (see page 169)	45	43
Fischer V G, 529 15th nw	46	45
FREE J D Jr, 1343 F nw (see page 163)	45	41
LANCASTER H C, 823 7th nw (Catholic—see page 169)	42	43
LEPLEY & FINSTER, 715 15th nw (Catholic—see page 170)	42	45
LOWDERMILK W H, 1424 F nw, U S Public Documents and antiquarian	45	45
WHITAKER G A, 1105 Pa av nw (see page 153)	49	43
WHITTINGTON J L, 1221 Pa av nw (see page 160)	47	43
nw	47	41
Bookbinders.		
WEIDMAN & WARNESON, 430 11th nw (see page 225)	48	43
Book Illustrations.		
COOLIDGE GEO A, 29 Corcoran bldg (see page 226)	46	45
Book Publishers.		
ARLINGTON PUBLISHING CO, 29 Corcoran Building (see page 221)	46	45
Boot and Shoe Makers.		
Ebsolf G, 1013 E nw	46	43
GEORGES J J, 1297 F nw (see page 226)	45	43
Iseman J S, 427½ 10th nw	47	41
Liedner N, 1726 Pa av nw	42	48
POTBURY & LEE, 1035 F nw (see page 174)	45	43
Vermillion J H, 616 9th nw	46	42
Young Wm, 1225 F nw	45	44
Boot and Shoe Stores.		
Dalton & Strickland, 939 Pa av nw	49	42
Edmonston A L, 913 Pa av and 1335 F nw	45	44
GEORGES J J, 1298 F nw (see page 226)	45	45
Hazleton A L, 428 7th nw	47	41
MILLER C P, 1025 7th nw (see page 156)	29	40
Moran A F, 1022 7th nw	29	40
Bottlers.		
ARLINGTON BOTTLING CO, 27th cor K nw (see p 141)	32	52
BRIDWELL M T, 325 M sw (see page 219)	64	38
Brass Works.		
Barbour & Mudhall, 802 E nw	46	42
DOUGLAS W H, 1224 D nw (see page 100)	48	44
Leitch R & Sons, 1214 D nw	48	44
Somerville T & Sons, 326 13th nw	49	44
Brewers.		
Goethler J O, D near 13th se	55	29
Heurich C, 1229 20th nw	30	46
Juenemann G Jr, 400 E ne	47	60
HARDY & WALSH (agents Phil. Bergner's Brewing Co, N Cap and G ne (see page 200)	44	36
Bricklayers.		
DAVIS A Jr, Corcoran building (see page 194)	46	45
Fitzpatrick J, 1216 N Y av nw	44	44
Foos J A, 807 D se	55	31
Goddard W W, 1836 7th nw	29	39
Miller J F, 823 1st se	48	36
Brokers—Real Estate.		
(See Real Estate Agents and Brokers.)		
Builders.		
(See Carpenters and Builders, also Contractors.)		
Builders' Materials and Supplies.		
Barker G W, 649 N Y av nw	39	40
Bird J H, 2002 H nw	44	43
Dunn R W, 5th and G ne	58	32
Hammond J R, 204 12th nw	59	43
McGill James H, 908-914 G nw	45	41
Thomas J A & Son, 1418 F nw	45	45
Cabinet Makers.		
Curry L, 6th c O nw	35	40
Dant J T & Son, 633 M nw	37	40
Grove A, 1204 N H av nw	29	45
Heitt W, 520 12th nw	46	44
Weaver J G & Son, 621 G nw	45	41
Carpenters and Builders.		
Anderson N, 629 14th nw	43	44
BROOKS J W Jr, 1107 C nw (see page 186)	46	48
Bright, Humphrey & Co, 1406 Pa av nw	46	45
Conrad F A & Son, 1218 E nw	46	43
Henderson J, 1211 E nw	46	43
LANGLEY & GETTINGER, 310 12th nw (see page 156)	56	43
Carpet Cleaners.		
Chace A H & Bro, 928 5th nw	41	39
Kline Lorenzo, 491 Mo av nw	57	40
Young F H, 15th K se and 1022 Pa av nw	47	45

	M.	T.
Carpet Dealers.		
(See also Furniture, &c.)		
Peterson & Childs, 833 Market Space nw	40	42
Carriage and Wagon Makers.		
WEAVER CLARENCE, 4½ and Pa av nw (see page 146)	51	40
Caterers.		
(See Confectioners.)		
China Decorators.		
HABENIGHT R, 334 Pa av nw (see page 165)	41	39
China, Glass, and Earthenware.		
Fololer J W & Son, 923 Pa av nw	49	41
SCHAEFER J W & BRO, 1020 7th nw (see page 186)	39	41
Watts G, 314 7th nw	47	41
Wilmarth & Edmonston, 1205 Pa av nw	48	44
Chiropodist.		
GEORGES J J, 1208 F nw (see page 220)	46	43
Cigars and Tobacco.		
BULKLEY E F, 706 K nw (see page 167)	48	41
Donnelly T, 5 Wholesale Row, Centre market	50	41
HENDERSON W A, 705 15th nw (see page 154)	45	45
LOUGHRAN D, 1413 Pa av nw (see page 151)	46	45
SCHULTZE J H, 2913 M nw (see page 164)	21	53
WETHERAL J W, 1201 F nw (see page 178)	46	43
Civil Engineers.		
LANG J C, 614 F nw (see page 246)	46	41
Clothiers.		
Eiseman Bros, 443 7th nw	47	41
Hollander J, 1217 Pa av nw	47	43
Kaufman C, 431 7th nw	47	41
Robinson B & Co, 909 Pa av nw	47	41
ROBINSON, PARKER & Co, c 7th and D nw (see page 204)	47	41
STRAUSS & MARX, 441 7th nw (see page 162)	47	41
Coal and Wood.		
CLARKE H A & SON, 933 F nw (see page 172)	45	42
Given J T, 423 10th nw	47	43
JOHNSON A G & BRO, M and 20th nw	31	48
Coal and Wood. Cont'd.		
LAMASON B P, 412 5th nw (see page 194)	43	40
MILLER J E & Co, 1300 F nw (see page 157)	46	44
Sheriff G L, 1115 Pa av nw	48	43
SMITH A B, 631 N Y av nw (see page 178)	39	40
Coffee Roasters.		
Browning T F, 232 3d nw	40	38
Lown W J, 7th c Md av sw	56	41
Sweeney J A, N J av c 3d nw	35	38
Coke Dealers.		
WASHINGTON GAS LIGHT CO, 10th nr D nw (see p 172)	45	45
Colleges.		
See Schools, Academies, Colleges, &c.; also Teachers.		
Commission Merchants.		
Anderson W S & Co, 921 B nw	51	42
Crawford J S & Co, 937 B nw	51	42
Davis J A & Son, 917 B nw	51	42
Drury W C & Co, 913 B nw	51	42
Magill C J, 909 B nw	51	42
Oyster G M & Co, Pa av cor 9th nw	50	42
YARDLEY CHAS, 906 10th nw (see page 197)	51	42
Confectioners and Caterers.		
(See also Bakers and Ice Cream Makers.)		
BUCKINGHAM F M & CO, 1223 Pa av nw (see page 165)	49	43
FLEISCHMANN C, 1410 Pa nw (see page 202)	47	45
HAILER W H, 811 14th nw (see page 158)	42	45
HERBERT H C, 440 9th nw (see page 179)	48	42
VELATI S, 620 9th nw (see page 161)	45	42
WEYMAN D J, 423 11th nw (see page 150)	46	43
WONN W W, 723 6th nw (see page 165)	45	41
Contractors.		
(See also Bricklayers, Carpenters, and Builders.)		
Argue, Carpenter & Co, 934 F nw	46	42
Barker J W, 65 Corcoran bldg	46	45
McGowan M A, 9 Corcoran bldg	46	45
McLAUGHLIN P H, Corcoran bldg (see page 216)	46	45
Morgan Thos P, 9 Corcoran bldg	46	45

	S.	T.
Contractors—Cont'd.		
Ross & Sanford, 1129 N Y av nw	43	45
WRIGHT CHAS. L. F (street sweeper patent machines), 1028 H nw (see page 227)	41	19
Costumers.		
Moxley Lloyd, 606 10th nw	44	33
Cracker Dealers.		
(See Bakers.)		
Dairies.		
(See Milk Dealers.)		
Dentists.		
BANCROFT S C, 914 F nw (see page 164)	46	42
Bliss E R, 1215 Pa av nw	47	43
Duke Y N, 715 13th nw	44	45
Crowton M B Jr, 906 F nw	46	42
McFarlan D, 1300 N Y av nw	42	44
Schaffhirt W C, 631 M nw	38	40
Detective Agency.		
McDevitt & Flinders, 605 Market space nw (see page 176)	50	17
Dining Rooms.		
(See also Restaurants.)		
BREUNINGER B L, 630 13th nw (see page 152)	45	44
EVANS FRED W, 923-931 F nw (see page 166)	48	42
GALE T P, 925 F nw (see page 166)	46	42
Smith C B, 912 F nw	46	42
TREWORTHY B T, Centre Market (see page 196)	50	41
Woodward & Milburn, 425 12th nw	47	43
Draughtsmen.		
Brown C W H, 620 F nw	46	40
Dieterich P C, 607 7th nw	46	41
Howard F W, 906 F nw	46	42
Kaiser J H, 633 F nw	45	39
Ormsd C H & F L, 709 G nw	45	40
Smallwood G T, 633 F nw	45	39
Dressmakers.		
Austen E, 1103 F nw	46	41
Ballenger M, 421 7th nw	47	41
Boggers J, 909 Pa av nw	48	44
CARUGHI-COOPER, MESDAMES & A MASON, 1010 F nw (see page 228)	46	43
Coffey Annie, 1116 Pa av nw	46	45
Druggists.		
BANCROFT R B, 1200 32d nw (see page 227)	18	54
GALE T P, 909 13th nw (see page 170)	12	43
COFFYNS & KIMPTON, 301 Pa av nw (see page 186)	54	30
Druggists—Cont'd.		
MERTZE E P, 1011 F nw (see page 161)	46	43
MILBURN J A, 1429 Pa av nw (see page 209)	46	45
MOORE P F, 1500 Pa av nw	43	47
PRICE C S, 426 7th nw (see page 171)	50	41
SIMMS G G C, cor 14th and N Y av, (see page 221)	48	45
THOMPSON W S, 703 15th nw (see page 155)	44	45
TYREE J S, 829 7th nw	48	41
WOODNUT J P, 1001 L nw	39	42
Dry Goods.		
BAUM CHAS, 416 7th nw (see page 149)	48	41
LANSBURGH & BRO, 420-426 7th nw (see page 190)	48	41
Dyers and Scourers.		
PRINCE WM, 1009 F nw (see page 222)	46	43
Electrical Apparatus.		
BOYCE & MORGAN, 1408 Pa av nw (see page 153)	47	45
Electrical Hair Remover.		
GABRIEL MRS DR, 614 12th nw (see page 190)	45	43
Electrotypers.		
(See also Stereotypers.)		
JOYCE MAURICE, 418 11th nw (see page 228)	48	43
Employment Bureaus.		
COOMBS & A, 205 F nw (see page 168)	40	82
DUNDORE L C & CO, 717 M nw (see page 209)	38	41
Engineers, Civil.		
(See Civil Engineers.)		
Engravers.		
HAAS G Jr, 1221 Pa av nw (steel—see page 165)	48	43
JOYCE M, 418 11th nw (general) (see page 228)	44	45
NICHOLS R B & CO, 902 F (wood—see page 203)	46	42
WANNER F J, 507 9th nw (glass—see page 203)	42	42
Expresses.		
Adams Express Co, 225 Pa av nw, 1425 F nw, and 6th cor Va av sw	51	38
Baltimore and Ohio, 629 and 1351 Pa av nw, N J av cor D nw, and 1002 331 nw	51	39

	N.	T.
Expresses—Cont'd.		
Knox's, 2d cor B nw, 603 Pa av nw, N Y av cor 35th nw, 1208 32d nw, and Pa av cor 2d se	50	38
SPRINGMANN & BRO, room 11 Post building, 1610 14th nw, 626 Md av sw, and S Cap cor D sw (see page 190)	40	42
MILLER J M & Co, 4th c H nw, 108 N L and 607 Center markets and Benning's road (see page 163)	44	39
Flour and Feed Dealers.		
Borns W G, 935 5th nw	42	37
Galt Wm M & Co, Ind av c 1st nw	49	38
Hewitt R C, 1225 7th nw	38	41
McDowell S C, Mass av c N Cap ne	46	37
Roth & Moore, 5th c K nw	42	37
Flower Embalmers.		
FRIES EVA, 909 8th nw (see page 181)	42	41
Furnaces and Stoves.		
BALL & SON C G, 1337 E nw (see page 206)	46	44
BUTLER'S STOVE EXCHANGE, 931 5th nw	42	40
SIMPSON & GUY, 1005 Pa av nw (see page 216)	48	43
Furniture, Upholstery, and Carpets.		
Brickwedde C A, 822 9th nw	43	42
GROGAN P, N Y av near 13th nw (see page 194)	43	44
Milne Alexander, 511 9th nw	46	42
Moses Wm B & Son, 1100 F nw	45	43
Slater J E, 704 A se	50	32
Williams Wash B, 317 7th nw	49	41
Gas-fitters.		
(See Plumbers and Gas-fitters)		
Gas Fixtures and Mantels.		
SHEDD S S, 409 9th nw (see page 202)	46	42
Gas-light Company.		
WASHINGTON GAS-LIGHT CO, 411 10th nw (see page 172)	48	40
Grocers.		
Abbott W E, 1721 Pa av nw	43	48
Barbour & Hamilton, 616 Pa av nw	50	41
Beall & Baker, 430 Pa av nw	51	40
Browning and Middleton, 610 Pa av nw	50	41
Bryan J H & Bro, 608 Pa av nw	50	41
Grocers—Cont'd.		
CORNWELL G G & SON, 1418 Pa av nw (see page 158)	47	45
EDMONSTON R O, 434 9th nw (see page 223)	47	42
Hume, Cleary & Co, 805 Market space	49	42
MAGRUDER J H, 1417 N Y av nw (see page 143)	43	45
Orme W & Son, 1013 Pa av nw	48	43
Walker & Wright, 948 La av nw	51	42
Gymnasium Home.		
RUEBSAM J E, 917 E nw (see page 142)	47	39
Hardware.		
Barber & Ross, 1004 Pa av nw	48	43
HARTIG L, 1406 14th nw (see page 200)	31	43
Lambie James B, 1413 N Y av nw	44	45
Schneider L H & Son, 1009 Pa av nw	48	43
Hair Dressers and Dealers in Human Hair.		
Demongeot M, 906 F nw	46	42
Kochon J, 507 13th nw	46	45
Wagner M, 1224 F nw	46	44
Harness and Saddles.		
(See Trunks.)		
Hats, Caps, and Furs.		
AUERBACH & BRO, 623 Pa av nw (see page 196)	50	41
DAVIS J Y SONS, 621 Pa av nw	50	41
KRAEMER H, 1020 7th nw (see page 195)	41	41
Stinemetz B H & Son, 1237 Pa av nw	48	43
Willett & Ruoff, 905 Pa av nw	50	42
Hotels.		
American, Pa av c 7th nw	50	41
ARLINGTON, Vt av c H nw	42	46
Belvidere The, Pa av c 3d nw	51	39
Carrollton, D c 8th nw	48	41
Chamberlin The, 831 15th nw	42	45
CLARENDON THE, N Y av c 14th nw (see page 209)	42	45
Clinton House, 826 7th nw	44	41
Congressional, 200 N J av nw	54	36
Dunbarton The, 628 Pa av nw	50	41
EBBITT HOUSE, F c 14th nw (see page 218)	46	44
EMMET HOUSE, N J av and C nw (see page 207)	49	37
Hamilton House, 14th c K nw	39	44
Howard House, 600 Pa av nw	50	40
McPherson House, 1423 I nw	41	45
Metropolitan The, 613 Pa av nw	50	41
National The, Pa av c 6th nw	51	40
RIGGS HOUSE, 15th c G nw	45	45

Hotels—Cont'd.

	N.	W.
SOLARIS, 1403 Pa av nw	47	45
ST CHARLES, c 3d and Pa av nw (see page 290)	51	39
St James, Pa av c 6th nw	51	40
St Marc, Pa av c 7th nw	50	41
Tremont House, 2d c Ind av	49	38
WELCKER'S, 725 15th nw	43	45
WILLARD'S, Pa av c 14th nw (see page 293)	47	45
WORMLEY'S, 1500 H nw	42	45

Ice Dealers.

	N.	W.
INDEPENDENT ICE CO, Pa av c 12th nw (see page 174)	48	43
TRANSPARENT ICE CO, 3213 Water, West Wash (see page 170)	16	56
WILLIS E M (Ice, Wharfage, and Stevedoring), Eldred wharf ss and railroad yard (see page 166)	61	43

Illustrations.

	N.	W.
COOLIDGE GEO A, 29 Corcoran bldg (see page 220)	46	45

Insect Powder.

	N.	W.
HART H I, 331 2d nw (see page 190)	45	38

Instrument Makers, Mathematical.

	N.	W.
Fauth & Co, 132 Md av sw	54	38
Hempler H H, 452 Pa av nw	51	40
Kubel E F, 226 1st nw	48	34
SHILLING G, 113 B se (see page 280)	56	34

Insurance Agents.

	N.	W.
Cross S, 916 Pa av nw	49	42
Dickson W, 224 4½ nw	49	40
Green O C, 200 7th nw	50	41
Lamer C N, 603 La av nw	49	40
Pratt A S & Sons, 601 9th nw	47	42

Insurance Companies, Fire (Local).

	N.	W.
COLUMBIA FIRE INSURANCE CO, H K Willard, sec, 1426 F nw	46	45
Corcoran Fire Insurance Co, 1001 F nw	46	42
German American Fire Insurance Co, 531 7th nw	48	42
Mutual Fire Insurance Co, 902 Pa av nw	50	42
National Metropolitan Fire Ins Co, 944 Pa av nw	50	42
Riggs Fire Insurance Co, 1331 F nw	46	44
Washington and Georgetown Firemen's Insurance Co, 7th and La av	50	41

Insurance Companies, Life (Local).

	N.	W.
Maryland Life Insurance Co, 519 7th nw	47	41
National U S A Life Insurance Co, 409 9th nw	46	42
National Life and Maturity Association, 1225 F nw	46	43
National Mutual Life Insurance Co, 1420 F nw	46	45
Valley Mutual Life Insurance Co, 1411 G nw	44	45
Washington Beneficial Endowment Ass'n, 931 F nw	46	42

Jewelers, Manufac'ring.

	N.	W.
Desio G, 1223 Pa av nw	47	43
Faber O G, 1114 D nw	49	42
Johannes J G, 935 Pa av nw	48	42

Kid Gloves.

	N.	W.
HIBBERT C H & Co, 941 Pa av nw (see page 216)	49	42

Kindling Wood.

	N.	W.
MILLER J E & CO, 13th c C nw (see page 157)	51	44

Lace Cleaners.

	N.	W.
Valmont Augustina, 1213 11th nw	27	44

Laces, Embroidery, &c.

	N.	W.
BAUM CHAS, 416 7th nw (see page 149)	48	41
Humphrey A K, 430 10th nw	48	43
Hutchinson, J C, 907 Pa av nw	50	42
Neet L, 415 13th nw	48	44
RUPPERT SELMA, 403 9th nw (see page 160)	46	42

Libraries.

(See Miscellaneous.)

Libraries, Circulating.

	N.	W.
FREE J D, 1343 F nw (see page 162)	45	44
Hunter L L, 1789 Pa av nw	42	46

Lime and Cement.

(See Builders' Materials.)

Lithographers.

(See also Photo-Lithographers.)

	N.	W.
COOLIDGE GEO A, agent, 29 Corcoran bldg (see page 220)	46	45
Kerrand J L, 1012 Pa av nw	49	43

Laundries.

	N.	W.
MORGAN J W, 517 9th nw (see page 142)	47	42

Lawyers.

(See Attorneys-at-Law.)

	M.	T.
Livery Stables.		
DRANEY F M, 443 K nw (see page 152)	41	39
LEADINGHAM & CO, 1327 H nw (see page 202)	43	44
NAILOR A Jr, 14th c E nw (see page 212)	48	44
PRICE J F & SON, 307-311 6th nw (see page 198)	49	43
Lock and Gun Smiths and Bell-hangers.		
Bargee S M, 626 D nw	48	41
Peabody J J, 717 D nw	48	41
Smith E H, 1104 E nw	46	45
Mineral Waters.		
BRIDWELL M T, 263 M sw (see page 219)	64	38
Lumber Dealers.		
McLean Wm R, 204 13th nw	51	44
Sheehan Geo A, 15th c B nw and 7th-street wharf sw	51	45
Smith Thos W, Ind av nw	50	38
Wheatley Bros, 3014 Water nw and 7th c K i av sw	31	54
Mail Contractors.		
ZEVERLEY A N & SON, 904 E nw	47	41
Mantels.		
ROCHE M, 493-497 C nw (see page 141)	49	40
Marble Workers.		
(See also Stone and Marble Yards.)		
BURNS & SON, 8 Cap and D sw (see page 223)	56	36
FLANNERY BROS, Del av c B sw (see page 147)	54	37
Markets.		
Boner S, 48 H nw	44	37
Brooke T S & Co, 1901 Vt av nw	38	44
Gheen Fred, 1928 Pa av nw	41	40
Neumyer E H, 1230 G nw	45	43
Oyster G M & Bro, 1106 12th nw	38	43
Tibbetts F J, 14th c N Y av nw	43	45
Massage.		
NISSEN H, 903 16th nw, Swedish Health Institute (see page 122)	30	46
Men's Furnishings.		
(See also Shirt Manufacturers.)		
Douglas & Bro, 326 9th nw	46	42
Franc H, 401 9th nw	48	41
IRELAND & WALSH, 1002 F nw (see page 180)	46	43
Men's Furnishings. Cont'd.		
KRAEMER H, 1026 7th nw (see page 176)	38	41
Tyssowski Bros, 701 15th nw	41	45
Milk Dealers.		
BREUNINGER H F, 618-620 13th nw (see page 150)	45	44
Rossell D B, 300 G nw	46	39
Wagner E, 403 E Cap nw	51	33
WARD F K, 929 D nw (see page 237)	40	42
Milliners and Millinery Goods.		
BAUM CHAS, 416 7th nw (see page 149)	48	41
Hunt M J, 1309 F nw	46	44
King M A, 1303 F nw	46	43
KING'S PALACE, 814 7th nw (see page 175)	43	41
Music and Musical Instruments.		
(See also Piano Fortes and Music.)		
DROOP E F, 925 Pa av nw (see page 209)	39	42
ELLIS J F & CO, 937 Pa av nw (see page 210)	40	42
METZEROTT W G & CO, 903 Pa av nw (see page 210)	40	42
WORCH H & CO, 923 7th nw (see page 148)	42	41
Musicians.		
Kaspar C, 1133 F nw	46	41
Lasby L E, 900 Pa av se	55	38
Pistorio N, 815 K se	56	38
Schroeder A W, 524 9th se	56	36
Newspapers.		
(See page 78.)		
Nurses.		
Washington Directory for Nurses, 832 13th nw	47	43
Out of Town.		
Schools, Colleges, Academies, &c.		
ARLINGTON INSTITUTE, Alexandria, Va, R C Powell, Principal (see page 179).		
MT VERNON ACADEMY, Alexandria, Va, A T L Kusian, Principal (see page 181).		
ST JOHN'S ACADEMY, Alexandria, Va, R L Carne, Principal (see page 187).		
ST MARY'S ACADEMY (Catholic) Alexandria Va, (see page 177).		

	P.	T.
Out of Town—Cont'd.		
UNION BRASS WORKS, 30 to 34 Plum st, Cincinnati (see page 211).		
WALPOLE DYE & CHEMICAL WORKS, 44 and 46 Oliver st, Boston (see page 244).		
WELLS J C, Electrician, 88 West Fayette st, Baltimore (over National Union Bank—see page 244).		
WHITTIER MACHINE CO, 1178 Tremont st, Boston, (see page 218).		
Painters, House and Sign.		
BROWN THOS A, 1413 F nw (see page 222)	45	45
MacNICHOL & SON, 415 10th nw (see page 220)	47	43
MILLER G W, 310 12th nw (see page 208)	42	43
Paints, Oils, &c.		
Rother W H, 900 C nw	50	40
Morgan J H, 908 G nw	45	42
SINEAL C J, 418 7th nw (see page 196)	48	43
Shanahan R, 1919 Pa av nw	41	49
Paper Dealers.		
Morrison E, 805-807 D nw	48	42
Paper-hangers and Hangings.		
DIETER L A, 913 F nw (see page 146)	46	42
DONN G S, 1225 7th nw	36	43
KRAUSE C A, 1225 N Y av nw (see page 231)	42	44
MARKRITER M J, 626 E nw	47	43
SEITZ C A, 1220 G nw (see page 180)	45	43
Patent Medicines.		
STARR Dr W M, 709 G nw (see page 164)	45	43
Patent Solicitors and Attorneys.		
BRADFORD R B, 721 G nw	45	43
DODGE & SON, 700 9th nw (see page 136)	44	42
EILS B E J, 703 7th nw (see page 172)	45	41
HALE F W, 812 F nw (see page 160)	46	42
HENDERSON W G, 925 F nw (see page 161)	46	42
HOUGH F H, 925 F nw (see page 151)	46	42
KNIGHT BROS, 633 F nw (see page 178)	47	43
McCLEARY & CHESNEY, 938 F nw (see page 170)	46	42

	S.	T.
Patent Solicitors and Attorneys—Cont'd.		
MURDOCK & MURDOCK, 1422 F nw (see page 192)	46	44
STODDART & CO, 503 B nw (see page 180)	44	40
WHITTLESEY & WRIGHT, 624 F nw, Pacific Building, (see page 218)	47	41
Photographers.		
MERRITT & VAN WAGNER, 935 Pa av nw (see page 195)	49	45
NATIONAL VIEW CO, 1126 Pa av nw (see page 219)	47	45
PARKER C, 477 Pa av (see page 154)	50	40
PULLMAN E J, 935 Pa av nw (see page 172)	48	42
Photo-Gravure & Photo Mechanical Printing.		
COOLIDGE GEO A, 214 Corcoran bldg (see page 226)	46	45
Photo-Lithographer.		
(See also Lithographers.)		
PETERS NORRIS, 458 Pa av nw (see page 126)	50	40
Photographic Materials.		
Cudlip C S & Co, 150 Pa av nw	51	40
Piano Fortes.		
(See Music Stores.)		
Plumbers and Gas Fitters.		
Hannan E J, 532 11th nw	46	44
Ragan J, 425 11th nw	47	43
Ridgway E A, 1311 F nw	46	44
SHEDD S S, 409 9th nw (see page 202)	47	42
Thorn C G, 1225 F nw	46	43
Printers, Book and Job.		
BROWN C W, 1319 F nw (see page 200)	45	44
CUREY A, 351 E nw (see page 190)	47	42
GIBBONS & BART, 635 7th nw (see page 174)	45	44
GRAY & CLARKSON, 770 Pa av nw (see page 232)	52	39
JUDD & DETWEILER, 420-422 11th nw (see page 231)	48	41
TOMLINSON J S, 632 F nw (see page 189)	46	41
Produce Dealers.		
(See Markets.)		
Publishers.		
ARLINGTON PUBLISHING CO, 20 Corcoran Building (see page 221)	46	45

	R.	T.
Real Estate Agents and Brokers.		
BATES & WHITMAN, 1407 F nw (see page 154)	45	45
DENISON W O, 923 F nw	45	42
HERTFORD J R, 1425½ F nw (see page 212)	46	41
MacLEWAN C M, 1340 F nw (see page 150)	45	41
MAIN W H, cor 3d and B nw (see page 233)	53	39
NORTH WASHING'N REAL ESTATE CO (Jos A Settle), 508-510 F nw (see page 145)	46	40
PITNEY & BRADFORD, 1313 F nw (see page 148)	46	40
PRESCOTT J A, 1416 F nw (see page 156)	46	45
RUFFIN R D, 1002 F nw (see page 150)	46	43
RYON & TRACY, 512 7th nw (see page 146)	47	41
SWORMSTEDT & BRADLEY, 927 F nw (see page 173)	45	42
TYLER & RUTHERFORD, 1225 F nw (see page 166)	45	44
YOUNG L C, 1407 F nw (see page 152)	45	45
Restaurants.		
(See also Dining Rooms.)		
GACHET L, 1424 Pa av nw (see page 173)	37	45
GASSENHEIMER S, cor Pa av and 6th nw (see page 222)	50	40
HARVEY G W, 1016 Pa av nw (see page 198)	48	43
KRAEMER C, 737 7th nw (see page 165)	44	41
POULTON W F, 227 7th nw	50	41
RUSSELL J H, 1430 N Y av nw (see page 206)	43	45
Schools, Academies, Colleges, and Seminaries.		
(See also Teachers.)		
"CEDARS THE," 1916 35th nw (see page 158)	6	53
CONVENT OF VISITATION, 1500 35th nw (see page 130)	9	54
EMERSON INSTITUTE, 914 14th nw (see page 206)	32	45
FRIENDS' SELECT SCHOOL, 1811 I nw (see page 204)	38	48
GEORGETOWN UNIVERSITY, head O nw (see page 166)	5	56
GONZAGA COLLEGE, 47 I nw (see page 154)	43	37
HOLY CROSS ACADEMY, Mass av bt 13th and 14th nw (see page 198)	36	44
KINDERGARTEN NORMAL INSTITUTE, 929 8th nw (see page 173)	38	41

	R.	T.
Schools, &c.—Cont'd.		
MT VERNON INSTITUTE, 1530 I nw (see page 182)	41	46
NORWOOD INSTITUTE, 1212 14th nw (see page 166)	35	44
SPENCERIAN BUSINESS COLLEGE, 9th cor D nw (see page 214)	48	41
ST CECELIA'S ACADEMY, 601 East Capitol (see page 200)	51	23
ST JOHN'S COLLEGIATE INSTITUTE, Vt av bt M and N nw (see page 170)	35	44
WASHINGTON ART SCHOOL, room 14 Vernon row, cor Pa av and 10th nw (see page 162)	49	42
Sculptors.		
BUHLER C W, 2207 Pa av nw (see page 185)	34	51
COLLIN & MOREAN, 715 14th nw (see page 181)	42	40
DUNBAR U S J, 318 2d sw (see page 198)	55	34
Sewing Machines.		
McKENNEY JAS F, 427 7th sw	49	51
Stamping Depot.		
BRASELMAN M E, 604 11th nw (see page 185)	45	43
Soap Makers.		
Mommert & Co, 25th c N nw	25	51
Kaub S C, B bt 13½ and 14th	52	44
Weaver, Kengla & Co, 3255 Water nw	25	36
Steamship Lines.		
(See also page 76.)		
Cunard Line, 605 7th nw	47	41
Inland Seaboard Coasting Co, foot of 6th sw	66	29
Mary Washington, foot of 7th sw	66	29
Maitano, foot of 7th sw	66	29
Mt Vernon Line, 7th st wharf	66	29
Potomac Steamboat Co, 7th st wharf	66	29
Potomac Transportation Line foot of 7th sw	66	29
Stenographers.		
LINNEY J J, 21 Corcoran bldg (see page 148)	46	45
Stereotypers.		
JOYCE, MAURICE, 416 11th nw (see page 228)	18	43
Stevedores.		
(See Wharfinger.)		

Stone and Marble Yards.

(See Marble Workers.)

	M	T.
ACKER & CO, N Cap c E nw (see page 210)	46	33
BENNER G L, 629 Mass av nw (see page 208)	62	41
GUBLER G W, 2?? Pa av nw (see page 180)	32	57
EVANS E, 1st and B sw (see page 221)	55	38
STEWART J & SON, 1314 9th nw (see page 177)	32	40
WALKER G S, 702 N Cap nw (see page 176)	44	37

Stoves, Ranges, &c.

	M	T.
Berry W H, 503 9th nw	46	42
Gatchell G E, 815 7th nw	62	42
O'Donnell W, 1248 7th nw	27	41
SIMPSON & GUY, 1005 Pa av nw (see page 210)	48	43
Wyvill W D, 432 Pa av nw	51	40

Swedish Health Institute.

(See also Massage.)

	M	T.
NISSEN H, 903 16th nw (see page 190)	41	46

Tailors.

	M	T.
ENGLISH J T, 719 15th nw (see page 156)	44	45
GRIESBAUER J A, 635 9th nw (see page 167)	48	42
HEROLD G W, 823 9th nw (see page 184)	42	42
KEST F W, 418 12th nw (see page 164)	47	43
SELTZ A G, 1312 F nw	46	41
SIEBEL & OWEN, N Y av c 15th nw (see page 171)	41	42

Teachers (Languages).

	M	T.
COLLIERE L E C, 1536 I nw (French Language—see page 166)	40	46
MYERS E H & L A FLINT, 1724 I nw (Languages—see page 208)	39	48

Teachers (Stenography).

	M	T.
MULVEY F J, 923 F nw (see page 189)	45	42
SPENCER L G, 9th c D nw (see page 185)	48	42

Telegraph Companies.

	M	T.
Baltimore & Ohio, 1351 Pa av nw	48	43
Mutual Union and Southern Telegraph Co, 1423 Pa av nw	46	45
Postal Telegraph and Cable Co, 1416 F nw	45	45
United Lines, 1428 F nw	46	45
Western Union, 531 15th nw	46	45

Telephone Companies.

	M	T.
Averell Insulating Conduit and Telephone, 1420 N Y av nw	44	45
Chesapeake and Potomac, 1420 N Y av nw	43	45
Long Telephone and Telegraph Co, 1334 F nw	46	44

Trunks.

	M	T.
Becker Conrad, 1315 Pa av nw	48	44
Knessi & Son, 425 7th nw	42	44
Topham J S, 1231 Pa av nw	47	43

Type-Writers.

	M	T.
Fracker John, 46 Corcoran building	46	45
Leech E M, 802 F nw	46	42

Type-Writing Machines.

	M	T.
PORTER W H, 931 F nw (Caligraph—see page 158)	45	42

Undertakers.

	M	T.
Burgdorf A, 316 Pa av nw	52	39
CARTER C K Jr, 3311 nw (see page 178)	43	39
GEIER FRANK'S SONS, 1113 7th nw (see page 163)	38	41
Speare W R, 940 F nw	46	42
Wright J R, 1337 10th nw	34	42

Upholsterers.

(See also Furniture Dealers.)

	M	T.
Atkinson G C, 627 H nw	44	41
Crampsey W M, 1002 F nw	46	43
JOHNS & ACKMANN, 1023 9th nw (see page 181)	39	41

Watches and Jewelry.

	M	T.
KARR J, 935 Pa av nw (see page 209)	50	41
LETMATE F W, 1336 F nw (see page 152)	46	41
SCHUERMANN E W & CO, 707 9th nw (see page 176)	44	42

Wharfinger.

	M	T.
WILLIS E M, foot of 13th sw (see page 163)	67	43

Window Shades.

(See Furniture, &c.)

Wines and Liquors.

	M	T.
FEGAN P (wholesale), 628 Pa av nw (see page 144)	51	40
KRAEMER C, 737 7th nw (see page 176)	44	43
MUEHLEISEN WM, 945 5th nw (see page 207)	43	40
XANDER C, 909 7th nw (see page 208)	42	41

Wood Dealers.

(See Coal and Wood.)

NEWSPAPER REPRESENTATIVES.

NEWSPAPER REPRESENTATIVES IN WASHINGTON.

Press Representatives entitled to Admission to the Press Galleries in Congress.

[For List of Washington Newspapers see page 78.]

N. Y. Associated Press—David R. McKee, Agent, Corcoran Bldg.
F. T. Bickford, Corcoran Building.
Jos. T. Brennan, Corcoran Building.
Eug. Davis, Corcoran Building.
Chas. J. Hayes, Corcoran Building.
Edw. M. Hood, Corcoran Building.
Western Associated Press—Chas. A. Boynton, Corcoran Building.
The United Press—P. V. DeGraw, 515 14th street.
W. W. Burham, 515 14th street.
W. E. Ringwalt, 515 14th street.

California.

California Associated Press—C. M. Ogden, 515 14th street n. w.
San Francisco Chronicle—G. Heazelton, 1405 F street n. w.
" Alta California—E. W. Ayres, 1420 N. Y. ave.

Colorado.

Denver Tribune—J. J. Noah, 1420 N. Y. ave.
" Republican— " "

Connecticut.

Hartford Times—John B. McCarthy, 248 3d street n. w.

District of Columbia.

Washington Post—W. S. Larner, 10th and D streets.
" " —Henry G. Eland, 10th and D streets.
" " —David Lewsley, 10th and D street.
Washington Critic—Wm. E. Ringwalt, 515 14th street.
Washington Star—F. P. Ferris, 1101 Pa. avenue.
" " —John P. Miller, 1101 Pa. avenue.
Washington National Republican—C. C. Riley, 10th and D streets.
" " —Louis Seibold, 10th and D sts.

Georgia.

Atlanta Constitution—F. H. Richardson, Metropolitan Hotel.
Atlanta Journal—W. F. Hinman, 1405 G street.
Augusta Chronicle—James R. Randall, 412 6th street.
Savannah News—H. B. F. Macfarland, 1420 Penna. ave.
" Times—R. M. Larner, 1314 F street.

ILLINOIS.

Chicago Daily News—Jules Guthridge, 1420 N. Y. avenue.
" Times—Fred. Perry Powers, 14th street and Pa. avenue.
" " —F. A. G. Handy, 513 14th street.
" " —John A. Corwin, 14th street and Pa. avenue.
" Tribune—Travis D. Wells, Corcoran Building.
" " —Chas. M. Pepper, Corcoran Building.
" Inter-Ocean—John M. Carson, 513 14th street.
" " —W. E. Curtis, 513 14th street.
" Herald—J. J. Noah, 1420 N. Y. avenue.
" Mail, 1424 N. Y. avenue.

INDIANA.

Indianapolis Times—Wm. J. Turpin, Hilman House.
" Sentinel—Jay F. Durham, 610 14th street.
" Journal—P. S. Heath, 513 14th street.

IOWA.

Sioux City Journal—L. B. Milton, 471 N. Y. avenue.
State Register—J. H. C. Wilson, 430 11th street.

KANSAS.

Kansas City Times—Edw. W. Ayres, 1420 N. Y. avenue.

KENTUCKY.

Louisville Post—O. P. Austin, 14th street and Pa. avenue.
" Courier-Journal—O. O. Stealey, 1343 F street.
" Times—Chas. E. Kincaid, 623 13th street.
Bowling Green Democrat—W. B. Dobson, 1239 G street.

LOUISIANA.

Times-Democrat—Richard Nixon, 1343 F street.
" —James W. Allison, 1343 F street.
New Orleans Picayune—L. Q. Washington, 1407 F street.

MAINE.

Portland Press—John L. Read, 1309 L street n. w.
Lewiston Journal— " " "
Portland Argus—Sherborne G. Hopkins, 736 8th street.
Bangor Commercial— " " "

MARYLAND.

Baltimore Times—Helena McCarty, 915 15th street.
" Sun—F. A Richardson, 1314 F street.
" " R. M. Larner, 1314 F street.
" " S. R. Flynn, 1314 F street.
" Herald—Franklin T. Howe, 515 14th street.
" American—John S. Schriver, 1420 Pa. avenue.

MASSACHUSETTS.

Boston Transcript—W. B. Shaw, Riggs House.
" Budget—Ben: Perley Poore, Ebbitt House.
" Globe—C. M. Ogden, 515 14th street.
" Post—C. F. Conant, 1420 New York avenue.
" Herald—Edmund Hudson, 1420 Pa. avenue.
" " H. B. F. Macfarland, 1420 Pa avenue.
" Journal—E. B. Wight, 1312 F street.
" Evening Record—F. D. Mussey, 511 14th street.
" Advertiser—R. J. Wynne, 511 14th street.
" Traveler—Chas. F. Towle, 1424 New York avenue.
" Newburyport Herald—Ben: Perley Poore, Ebbitt House.

MICHIGAN.

Detroit News—David S. Barry, 1234 13th street.
" Tribune—Ernst E. Russell, 1427 F street.
Saginaw Courier—Geo. R. Robertson, 1315 C street n. w.

MINNESOTA.

Minneapolis Tribune—Chas. A. Hamilton, 1420 Pa. avenue.
St. Paul Pioneer Press—Charles H. Gray, 515 14th street.

MISSOURI.

St. Louis Post Dispatch—Geo. G. Bain, 610 14th street.
" Westliche Post—L. W. Habercom, 515 14th street.
" Globe Democrat—Walter B Stevens, 511 14th street.
Missouri Republican—Chas. W. Knapp, 1407 F street.
St. Louis Chronicle—Harry M. Chapman, 1427 F street.

NEBRASKA.

Omaha Herald—Geo. E. Earle, 1427 F street.

NEW JERSEY.

State Gazette—Geo. O. Glavis, 515 14th street.
Jersey City Daily Argus—J. Walter Mitchell, 111 D street s. w.
Newark News—J. Walter Mitchell, 111 D sw.

NEW YORK.

Tribune—M. G. Seckendorff, 1322 F street.
" S. N. Clark, 1322 F street.
Times—E. G. Dunnell, 515 14th street.
" Frank A. De Puy, 515 14th street.
Evening Post—E. B. Wight, 1312 F street.
Morning Journal—615 14th street.
Sun—A. W. Lyman, 507 14th street.
Staats Zeitung—Paul Wolff, 1351 Pa. avenue.
World—T. C. Crawford, 610 14th street.
Journal of Commerce—Thos. B. Kirby, 14th and Pa. avenue.

NEW YORK—Cont'd.

Star—O. O. Stealey, 1343 F street.
" Edson C. Brace, 1343 F street.
Commercial Advertiser—C. S. Elliot, 507 15th street.
Herald—Chas. Nordhoff, 15th and G streets.
" Herbert A. Preston, 701 15th street.
" Julius Chambers, 15th and G streets.
Commercial Bulletin—Wm. E. Ringwalt, 515 14th street.
Telegram—Chas. F. Towle, 1424 N. Y. avenue.
Brooklyn Standard—W. F. Hinman, 1405 G street n. w.
" Eagle—A. Burton, 1424 N. Y. avenue.
" Union—Frank P. Morgan, 1424 N. Y. avenue.
" Times—Chas. A. Hamilton, 1420 Pa. avenue.
Buffalo Express—Chas. A. Hamilton, 1420 Pa. avenue.
" Times—C. P. Hunt, 515 14th street.
Troy Times—C. P. Hunt, 515 14th street.
Albany Evening Journal—Ben: Perley Poore, Ebbitt House.

NEW HAMPSHIRE.

Nashua Telegram—F. A. Moore, 317 East Capitol street.
Portsmouth Daily Times—Jos. F. Pagaud, 76 Harlem ave., Balto.

NORTH CAROLINA.

Charlotte Observer—Cicero W. Harris, 1507 Vermont avenue.

OHIO.

State Journal—P. S. Heath, 513 14th street.
Cincinnati Commercial Gazette—Rob. G. Wynne, 511 14th street.
" " H. V. Boynton, 14th and Pa. ave.
Cincinnati Inquirer—W. C. MacBride, 14th street and Pa. avenue.
" " G. E. Gilliland, 14th street and Pa. avenue.
" Times—O. P. Austin, 14th street and Pa. avenue.
Cleveland Leader—Frank G. Carpenter, 1427 F street.
" " Geo. H. Walker, 1427 F street.
" Penny Press—David S. Barry, 1224 13th street.
" Plain Dealer—L. C. MacPherson, 14th street and Pa. ave.
Toledo Evening Post—W. B. Dobson, 1239 G street.
Steubenville Herald—W. G. Lampton, 525 11th street.
Columbus Times—L. C. MacPherson, 14th street and Pa. avenue.

OREGON.

The Oregonian—T. C. Judkins, 620 11th street.

PENNSYLVANIA.

Philadelphia Times—Chas. T. Murray, 515 14th street.
" Press—C. M. Ogden, 515 14th street
" Evening Star—James R. Young, 1506 Q street n. w.
" Inquirer—U. H. Painter, 900 14th street.
" Evening Bulletin—1427 F street.

PENNSYLVANIA—Cont'd.

Philadelphia Telegraph—507 14th street.
" Record—H. B. F. Macfarland, 1420 Pa. avenue.
" Ledger—J. M. Carson, 513 14th street.
Pittsburg Telegraph—Geo. Martin, 515 14th street.
" Dispatch—Chas. T. Murray, 515 14th street.
" Post—Thos. C. Hannum, 14th street and Pa. avenue.
Harrisburg Telegraph—DeB. Randolph Keim, 607 M street.

SOUTH CAROLINA.

Charleston News and Courrier—Rob. M. Larner, 1314 F street.

TENNESSEE.

Nashville American—E. B. Wade, 9th street n. w.
" Republican—C. C. Riley, 10th and D streets.
Memphis Appeal—H. W. Spofford, 1420 Pa. avenue.

TEXAS.

Galveston News—Wm. A. Fields, House Rep., Clerk's Office.

UTAH.

Salt Lake Tribune—T. B. Kirby, 513 14th street.

VIRGINIA.

Alexandria Gazette—Harold Snowden, Alexandria.
Richmond State—Alfred J. Stofer, 930 T street.
" Dispatch—R. F. Howard, 610 C street n. e.

WEST VIRGINIA.

Wheeling Intelligencer—Geo. A. Dunnington, 1203 11th street.

WISCONSIN.

Milwaukee Herald—E. W. Habercom, 515 14th street.
" Sentinel—Frank Markel, 1220 H n. w.

ILLUSTRATED

COMMERCIAL REGISTER.

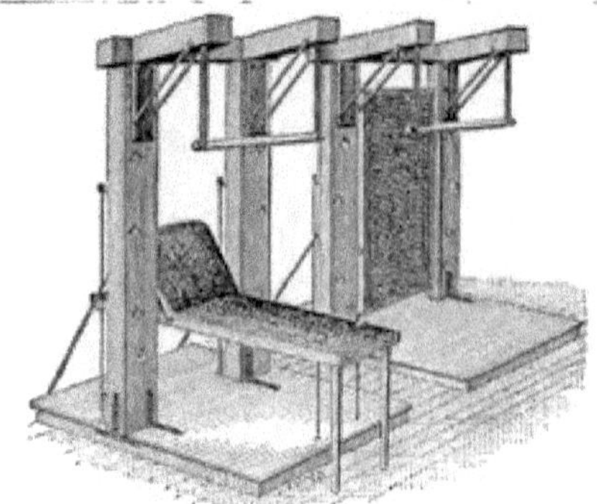

THE SWEDISH HEALTH-INSTITUTE.

From a modest introduction in this city, a few years ago, of this important method of restoring health, it has merited popularity to the extent of necessitating accommodation at 903 16th street N. W., in well furnished and equipped parlors on two different floors. The treatment is administered between 8 a. m. and 8 p. m., by Hartvig Nissen, the Proprietor and Director, with an efficient corps of assistants. He also treats patients at their homes, if desired.

The method of this system of dealing with disorders to which mankind is subjected, is not generally known although of ancient origin—hence it is considered of mutual benefit to offer a short description of its process. It has existed in all ages because it is based on mechanical and anatomical principles, and produces salutary effects when other remedies are not applicable.

The name of Swedish Health Institute is derived from what is known as the Swedish Movement Cure, combined with Massage. As Linnaeus systematized botany, Berzelius chemistry, so did another Swedish professor, Pehr Henrik Ling, in 1813, establish an everlasting repution by effecting astonishing cures through manipulation of the human body without employment of medicine.

He organized a Central Institute, now supported by the Swedish Government in Stockholm, from which graduates have established others in almost every country in the civilized world.

The system of the Swedish Movement Cure deals mainly with the circulation of the blood—a part of physiology not much known until about the middle of the seventeenth century.

Visitors are always welcome to inspect the institute and examine the mode of treatment.

AN ENTIRE FOUR-STORY BUILDING

DEVOTED TO HANDLING

IMPORTED AND DOMESTIC

GROCERIES,

WINES,

CHAMPAGNES, LIQUORS, CIGARS, &c.

JOHN H. MAGRUDER,

1417 NEW YORK AVE.,

NEAR U. S. TREASURY.

MORGAN'S
STEAM LAUNDRY.
GLOSS OR DOMESTIC FINISH
COLLARS and CUFFS
TROY STYLE.
517 NINTH STREET N. W.

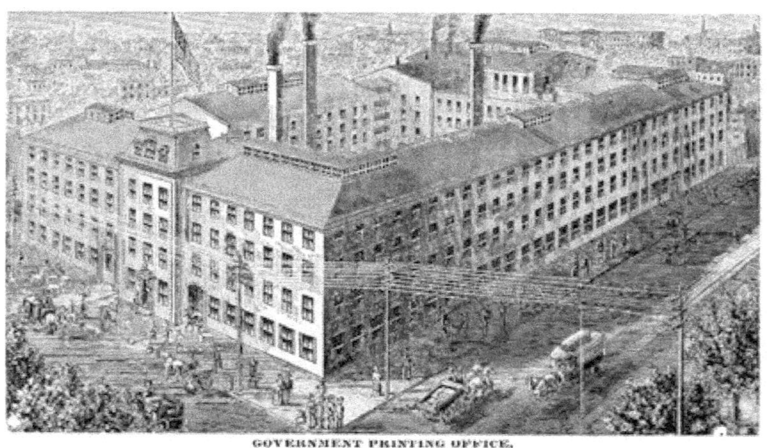

GOVERNMENT PRINTING OFFICE.

CAPITOL—East Front.

Washington Real Estate has been clearly demonstrated to be the very best of investment in the country—many large fortunes have grown from small beginnings in this kind of property. Any wanting homes or investments can find such as they desire at the North Washington Real Estate Co., 508 and 510 F street N. W.

Photography in Washington has reached the highest grade of achievement in the Gallery of Messrs. Merritt and Van Wagner, 925 Pennsylvania avenue, headquarters for Cabinets, Boudoirs, and Panels of all sizes, Crayons, Portraits, etc. Outside groups are taken and unmounted views furnished for insertion in albums. Mr. Merritt has himself made over 30,000 sittings in this gallery alone, which testifies to his high professional skill and popularity. He is very successful in photographing children, for which the facilities of this gallery are unsurpassed. Their rooms have an historic interest as those formerly used by the "Shepherd Ring." Here also the great picture of the "Electoral Commission" was painted by Mrs. Fassett. A fine collection of new and picturesque views of the city are now on sale here.

CAPITOL—West Front.

The improvements in the Capitol Building and Grounds have been placed in charge of Fred. Law Olmstead, the talented New York architect.

Messrs. Flannery Bros., to whom have been entrusted the execution of the improvements of the Capitol Building, represented in the above illustration, are an enterprising firm of Contractors located at the corner of Delaware Avenue and B Street S. W., opposite the south front of the Capitol. They own extensive Marble and Granite Works and have achieved an enviable reputation for rare and choice designs in Artistic and Monumental Memorials. For many years the members of the firm have resided in Washington and have been extensively employed by the U. S. Government and by prominent citizens from all parts of the country in work of the highest grade with entire satisfaction. Correspondence for Cemetery and Contract work is guaranteed special attention. Every courtesy is extended to the public.

WHITE HOUSE—Front View.

One of the largest and perhaps the most complete establishment of its kind in this city is the Dry Goods, Millinery, and Notions Stores of Mr. Charles Baum, located on Seventh, Eighth, and D streets northwest. This gentleman's career as a merchant of Washington has been most eventful as well as exceptionally successful. He came here at the close of the civil war, aspiring to establish a first-class business, though then possessing literally but one penny of capital. Pluck, perseverance, and business capacity did the rest. From a small rented room Mr. Baum's business has steadily increased until it now occupies the commodious stores which are so well known to and appreciated by the local public. A specialty of his has been to procure his stock for the various seasons with the energy displayed by the leading merchants of the East, and to conduct the sales at the lowest rates. The ladies appreciate how complete and how well furnished with the latest novelties is the millinery and notion department of this enterprising house.

WHITE HOUSE—North Front.

The Wholesale and Retail Cigar and Tobacco establishment of Daniel Loughran is located at 1413 Pennsylvania Avenue, a few doors above Willard's Hotel, where goods of the finest quality can always be found. Mr. Loughran supplies a large trade in this city.

Fronting on the beautiful McPherson Square, and conveniently near the chief points of interest in the city, is Chamberlain's far-famed Hotel, which has been the scene of so many public and private festivities in the social world of Washington. Here a delicious *menu* is always served, in a manner which does credit to the Capital. The apartments also are of ample proportions, and artistically decorated. Families desiring to make a short stay in the city can there avoid the crowds and confusion which characterize the larger Hotels during "the season." For gentlemen the large café at Chamberlain's affords a delightful place for the interchange of the latest social news and political ideas—almost equal to a Casino. Notwithstanding all the recent competition Chamberlain's thrives and even increases in popularity, as it deserves to do.

WHITE HOUSE—Rear View.

A complete stock of Books, Stationery, Visiting Cards, &c., can always be found at the Large Store of Mr. Grenville A. Whitaker, 1105 Pennsylvania Avenue N. W. This Establishment is worthy of the large patronage which it is continually receiving.

Mr. Henry Beard, 925 F Street N. W., Land Claim Attorney, practices in the Courts of the United States, Interior Department, and General Land Office. The principal business of Mr. Beard is that of adjusting Railroad Land Grants. He has frequently been engaged in very important cases of this kind before the Interior Department.

Bladensburg is an old town, famous for being a hundred years ago the largest commercial city in Maryland. At present it is a quiet, picturesque, country village.

Franklin H. Hough, Counselor-at-Law and Solicitor of American and Foreign Patents, 925 F Streets N. W., near U. S. Patent Office, makes a speciality of procuring Patents, Copyrights, &c. Trade Marks and Labels Registered. Send to him sketch or model for free Opinion as to Patentability. All correspondence promptly answered.

TREASURY—Pennsylvania Avenue and 15th Street.

F. M. Buckingham & Co., Manufacturers of Pure Confections, 1223 Pennsylvania Avenue, have a fine and well-stocked store, from which they supply a large trade throughout the city. They are noted for the purity of their Confections. A Branch Store is conducted at Asbury Park.

Mr. W. S. Thompson, Pharmacist, is probably the best known gentlemen of his profession in this city. His store is located at 703 Fifteenth Street N. W., near New York Avenue and opposite the Treasury Building, and is always stocked with the Purest and Finest Goods in the Market. With an efficient corps of clerks, and always present at his place of business, his success has been assured.

During the past winter much interest has been shown by citizens of Washington in taking steps to have a permanent Industrial Exhibition located at the Capital. A committee of influential citizens has been appointed to forward the movement.

STATE, WAR, AND NAVY DEPARTMENTS.

The coal business of Washington, D. C., has become one of very large proportions. The firm of James E. Miller & Co., wholesale and retail dealers in coal and wood, whose office, yard, and factory are located corner of Fourteenth and C streets N. W., and who also have an office No. 1300 F street, corner Thirteenth street N. W., have always on hand the largest stock of best mined and most carefully selected Anthracite, Cannel, Splint, and Bituminous Coal in the city, and all stored under cover, so that coal ordered from this firm, even in the most inclement weather, is delivered dry and clean. Coal by the ton, car, or cargo at the very lowest market rates—2,240 lbs. to the ton, and 128 cubic feet to the cord.

All kinds of wood by the cord, car, or vessel load, and also in bundles, sawed and split by the best and most improved machinery—kept under cover.

Orders sent by mail or telephone will in all cases receive prompt attention by the above firm.

G. G. CORNWELL & SON, Agts.

DUMINY EXTRA SEC.

THE LEADING CHAMPAGNE.

BRANDENBURG FRERES' CLARETS, WHITE WINES AND OLIVE OIL.

C. Lauteren Sohn, Rhine Wines. R. Bruninghaus Burgundies.

G. G. CORNWELL & SON,

Fine Family Groceries,

OLD WINES, BRANDIES, WHISKIES, ETC.

HAVANA CIGARS.

Nos. 1416 and 1418 Pennsylvania Avenue,

OPPOSITE WILLARD'S HOTEL.

WASHINGTON, D. C.

NATIONAL ACADEMY OF FINE ARTS.

The most thorough instruction in every department of Art, from the Preparatory Course to Portrait and Historical Painting, on the most reasonable terms. Instruction in classes, or private lessons, for children, young persons, and middle-aged ladies and gentlemen. Years of study saved. Mrs. IMOGENE ROBINSON MORRELL, the founder and teacher, has had twelve medals, and studied fifteen years in Europe with the most celebrated artists.

CORNER OF 7TH AND E STREETS N. W. WASHINGTON, D. C.

HAILER'S

Fancy • Bakery • and • Confectionery,

AND CAFÉ,

811 FOURTEENTH STREET N. W.

ICE CREAM AND ICES. CHARLOTTE RUSSES. JELLIES.
WEDDING CAKES A SPECIALTY.

CORCORAN ART GALLERY.

The beautiful architecture of Washington is a noticeable feature of the city. More important to owners and inmates, however, than exterior effect, is thoroughness in construction and honesty and skill in interior workmanship. A firm which have rapidly established a reputation for the best class of work, at reasonable rates, are Messrs. Langley & Gettinger, the Builders and Carpenters, whose office is at No. 310 12th Street N. W. In busy times they employ a large corps of workmen. The firm accepts contracts for erecting and completing all classes of buildings, ready for occupancy. A large jobbing and repairing business is also carried on, under the personal supervision of the proprietors. The best proofs of their competence and popularity are the buildings which have recently been built by these men, in coöperation with the various leading architects of this city. References, by permission, to many leading citizens.

PATENT OFFICE.

Queen Anne Cologne is unequalled by any in the market, imported or domestic. Put up in handsome pint bottles at $1.00 per bottle. Manufactured and always for sale by Edward P. Mertz, the well known Family Chemist and Druggist, 1014 F Street, corner 11th, N. W.

A reliable Patent Attorney is William G. Henderson, 925 F Street N. W. He has served many years in the Patent Office, and gained an intimate knowledge of its workings. He is a member of the Bar of the Supreme Court of the United States, and has an established reputation for ability, learning, and devotion to the interests of his clients.

Velati's Confectionery Store, 620 9th Street, near U. S. Patent Office, is noted for its famous Caramels, made fresh every day; also the finest Fruits of the season, and exquisite Confections. A Branch Store is also successfully conducted at 1706 Pennsylvania Avenue N. W.

POST OFFICE BUILDING.

The Book and Stationery Store of D. A. Brosnan, 612 9th Street N. W., always contains a full supply of Catholic Literature, Candles and Oil for Church purposes, Rosaries, Crucifixes, Medals, &c. D. A. Brosnan is also an European Passage Agent.

Washington is already noted for its "summer opera"—an innovation which was commenced here some years ago. New light operas may be seen here for the marvelously low price of twenty-five cents. They are largely patronized by the best class of people.

Brightwood is a pleasure resort about four miles north of the city. It has a good hotel and is reached by the Fourteenth-street and Seventh-street roads, affording an enjoyable drive. This drive is much frequented.

The finest Cut Flowers and Budding Plants are kept constantly on hand at the corner of 4th Street and Massachusetts Avenue N. W., by John Miller & Co., Florists. They also occupy stands Nos. 108 and 110, Northern Liberty Market. Their extensive Green Houses are located on Benning's road.

DOCTOR STARR'S

CELEBRATED

COUGH SYRUP,	LIVER PILLS,
(Cures Coughs, Colds and Group.)	(Cures Biliousness, Headache and St. Vitus Dance.)

AND KIDNEY TEA,

(Cures Kidney and Back Troubles.)

CHILLS AND FEVER TEA.

Each Preparation 25 cts.

Manufactory, 709 G Street N. W.

Prescriptions used are all composed of best Herbs, gathered by Dr. Starr, and utilized to the entire satisfaction of all who try his genuine compounds. All preparations, excepting Cough Syrup, can be sent by mail, postpaid, to any part of the country or Europe. Circulars sent free.

JOHN H. SCHULTZE,

—MANUFACTURER OF—

FINE HAVANA CIGARS

—AND DEALER IN—

LEAF TOBACCO,

2913 *M STREET, WEST WASHINGTON.*

F. W. REST,

MERCHANT TAILOR,

418 TWELFTH STREET N. W.

$5.00 Pants Made to Order, a specialty.

PENSION OFFICE.

A rapidly rising tradesman is Mr. George Haas, Jr., Engraver and Plate Printer, 1221 Pennsylvania Avenue. Engraving of every kind and description is carried on, such as Visiting, Reception, Wedding and Business Cards, in fact anything from a Card to a Bank note. The excellence of his work is his commendation.

Those wishing Refreshments will do well to visit the Confectionery of Mr. W. W. Wonn, No. 721 Sixth Street N.W. Mr. Wonn is a Baker, Confectioner, and Ice Cream Manufacturer, and prides himself upon the excellence of his stock.

Within the past few years the large tract of land lying to the south of the President's House has been reclaimed. Improvements are now in progress, which when completed will render this a handsome riverside park two and one-half miles long, and will beside add materially to the health of the city. This is a public work, which the Members of Congress cannot afford to neglect, as its feasibility at a very moderate outlay has been practically demonstrated by competent authorities.

SMITHSONIAN INSTITUTION.

One of the best Tailors of Washington is Mr. J. A. Griesbauer, 435 Ninth Street near E, N. W., where Tailoring in all its branches is done in the best manner. Style and fit, as well as durability of goods, are guaranteed at reasonable prices.

Rowing has been cultivated to a high degree at the National Capitol. The Boat Clubs are in a most flourishing condition with a full membership, several of them owning Club Houses which are not excelled anywhere in the country. All classes and descriptions of racing and pleasure boats are in constant use by the members and their guests. Frequent and exciting regattas keep up the interest and perfect the grade of oarsmanship. The leading clubs are the Columbias, Potomacs, Analostans, Capitols, and Washingtons, all located in West Washington. Elegant and safe boats may be hired by visitors at the Boat Houses of Cumberland & Son, and Passeno, at the foot of 32d Street, West Washington.

NATIONAL MUSEUM.

St. Mary's Academy, Alexandria, Virginia, is an Institution for Boarding and Select Day Pupils. This school opens on the first Tuesday in September and closes the last week in June. Special attention is paid to Music, Painting, and Drawing. By applying to the Sister Superior full particulars will be given. Parents who place their children here may be sure that they will receive an excellent education.

One of the most interesting objects to visitors at the Capitol is the Panorama of the Battle of Manassas, or Second Bull Run. It is located in a very commodious and convenient brick structure on the corner of Ohio Avenue and Fifteenth Street N. W. The scenes are painted by Theo. Poilpot who is also the author of the best Panoramas both abroad and in this country, and there is here presented a wonderful optical illusion as well as a most realistic battle scene. The building is open from 9 a. m. till 12 p. m.

ARMY MEDICAL MUSEUM.

Siebel & Owen, Merchant Tailors, corner New York Avenue and 10th Street N. W. are well known throughout the city for their integrity in business and the superior character of their work. Always ready to meet any demand, prompt in filling their orders, they are entitled to the patronage of all who are seeking services in their line.

Mr. C. S. Price, the enterprising Pharmacist, 426 Seventh Street S. W., has enlarged his store and increased his general stock to meet the demands of his many patrons. With him, "Quality is of the first importance in medicine, prescriptions the specialty."

The proposed Rock Creek Park extends along a picturesque valley, through which a stream flows towards the Potomac. Diversified by bold hills, and well wooded, this beautiful tract of land may very easily be transformed into one of the most lovely parks imaginable. Civil Engineers have made calculations that this can be done at a reasonable outlay. Nothing would be more acceptable to the citizens of Washington than to see this magnificent country utilized, as the Park would be so near the city as to afford health and recreation to thousands during all seasons of the year.

AGRICULTURAL BUILDING.

The Washington Kindergarden Normal Institute, Mrs. Louise Pollock, Principal, is located at 929 Eighth Street N. W. Training of Teachers; Course eight months.

Free Kindergarden Training School for nurses and governesses, Mrs. Louise Pollock, Superintendent, located S. E. corner of Eighth and K Streets N. W. School course, twelve weeks.

Restaurant De Paris, 1424 Pennsylvania Avenue, opposite Willards Hotel, Louise Gatchet, Proprietor, will serve private dinners and parties outside at short notice. Table D'Hote and à La Carte all day. Boarders at very reasonable rates.

About ten years ago the National Jockey Club, composed of representative business men of Washington and its vicinity, located a fine race track and fair grounds at Ivy City, about two and a half miles from Washington, on the Baltimore and Ohio Railroad. The venture has proved a decided success.

BUREAU OF ENGRAVING AND PRINTING.

The largest millinery and cloak house in the District is that of H. King, Jr., known as King's Palace, located at 817 Seventh Street Northwest, and extending back through the entire square, having a frontage on Eighth street. Here can be found in profusion all the latest styles of Ladies', Misses', and Children's Trimmed and Untrimmed Hats. Flowers of every description, Ribbons of all hues and qualities, Laces, imported and domestic, Silks from the highest to the ordinary grades, Velvets of the most superior quality, Tips, Plumes, Parasols, Lace Caps, Cloaks for Ladies, Misses and Children.

Mr. King is so well known that the mention of his "Palace" as the place to obtain what is required banishes all doubt, and his able Corps of Assistants are constantly kept busy supplying the hundreds of customers who visit his store daily. By earnest application to business and strictest integrity this establishment has been enlarged and extended until now its manager can offer rare bargains.

WASHINGTON MONUMENT.

The Granite and Soft Stone Works of J. Stewart are located on New York Avenue, between Fourth and Fifth Streets N. W. Mr. Stewart makes a specialty of fine Monumental work, and has had a large experience.

ARLINGTON HOUSE.

H. C. Herbert, 440 Ninth Street N. W., is noted for the Manufacture of Fine Cakes and Superfine Bon-Bons, which are always in demand. His Establishment is one of the finest in the city. Mr. Herbert is a most enterprising and reliable business man.

Schuetzen Park, one of the most attractive Pleasure Parks in the vicinity of Washington, is situated on Seventh Street extended, in the vicinity of Soldier's Home. It occupies a large tract of handsomely improved grounds, and has a commodious Club House for the use of members. This is a favorite resort for pleasure parties, and is open to the public on all days, except Sundays.

Congress has now under consideration a plan for completing a topographical survey of the district, delineating the extension of certain street and avenues, especially in the northern and western portion of the city. No city in the country stands more in need of a liberal policy in such matters than Washington.

MOUNT VERNON.

Among the representative business men of Washington is Mr. George W. Herold, Merchant Tailor, 824 Ninth Street N. W. Mr. Herold is one of the most successful Fitters in this city, and has always on hand as fine a lot of goods as any establishment of this kind.

Mrs. Fries, 909 Eighth Street N. W., is an expert in the Preservation of Bridal and Funeral Designs in Wax, and guarantees the original Flowers. Hair work on Glass and Pearl. References: Mrs. U. S. Grant, W. W. Corcoran, General Casey, and General Aiken.

Mount Vernon Institute, located at 42 South Washington Street, Alexandria, Virginia, is a Boarding and Day School for Young Ladies. The Principals are A. T. L. Kussian, LL.D., and Miss Mary A. Roach, with an efficient corps of teachers.

Dr. S. C. Bancroft, Dentist, 914 F Street N. W., is a graduate of Harvard Dental College, having many years of practical experience. Dr. Bancroft's office is perfectly equipped with all the appliances for use in his profession.

SOLDIERS' HOME.

The Fine Undertaking Establishment of Frank Geier's Sons, is located at 1113 Seventh Street N. W. The firm is composed of Joseph B. and Joseph A. Geier, who take great pride in guaranteeing their work as strictly first-class and at very moderate prices.

The firm of McCleary & Chesney, Patent Solicitors, No. 938 F Street N. W., near the Patent Office, are commended to the public as reliable Solicitors of high standing. Send to them for information relative to inventions or Patents.

A novelty is the new system of baggage delivery begun by the Pennsylvania Railroad Company last May, and which has been largely patronized by the public. Under this system by prepaying one dollar any traveler may have his trunk sent on in advance and delivered at the desired destination without further care on his part.

PRESIDENT'S COTTAGE.

Clinton A. Seitz, 1229 G Street N. W., is not only a practical Paper-Hanger but has always on hand in his store a full supply of Wall-papers, Curtains, and Picture Frames. Terms very reasonable.

Opposite the Washington Circle, 2307 Pennsylvania Avenue N. W., will be found the Sculptor and Modeler, Mr. C.W. Bühlor, who will furnish Models, Estimates, and Drawings, upon application, for all kinds of Marble and Granite work. Specialty, Church Altars, Fonts, &c.

Mrs. E. Braselman, Teacher of Art and Needle-work, 604 Eleventh Street N. W., is also dealer in Fine Decorative Art Embroidery Materials. A full line of Stamped and Unstamped Linen and Cotton goods always on hand. Designs for Lustro and Kensington Painting.

The only place in the city where the Firing, Gilding, and Decorating of Porcelain and Stone China can be done at moderate prices is the establishment of Robert Habenight, China Decorator, 334 Pennsylvania Avenue N. W. A Specialty is the Decoration of Barber's mugs.

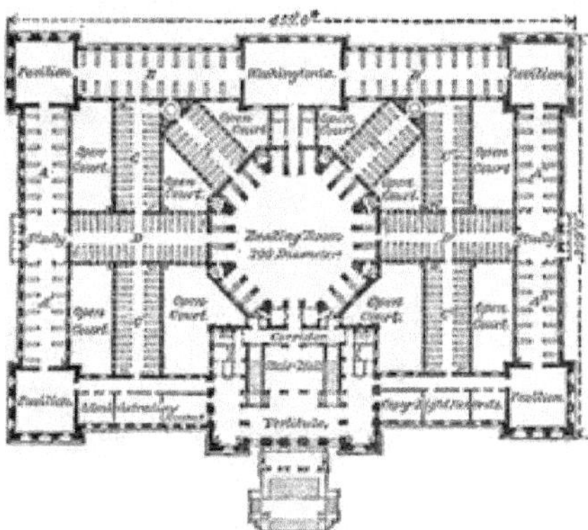

LIBRARY GROUND PLAN.

Among the prominent Architects of this city is the firm of Smithmeyer & Pelz, the designers of the New Congressional Library Building, a plan of which is given above. Many evidences of their work are to be found throughout this city and country, among which may be mentioned the Georgetown College, the annex to the U. S. Post Office Building, and many of the handsomest residences in the city, including that of Lieutenant Emory, General Cutter, and Mr. Holliday. Their plan for the Congressional Library was selected through public competition, and received the first premium.

Mr. J. L. Smithmeyer was born in Vienna, Austria. He is the author of "Library Architecture," a book embodying the result of an extended tour of inspection through Europe. Mr. P. J. Pelz was born in Silesia, Germany, receiving his collegiate education in Breslau, and his professional education in New York.

NEW LIBRARY BUILDING.

J. S. Tomlinson, Book and Job Printer, 632 F Street N. W., Federal Building, can supply at shortest notice all kinds of Book, Pamphlet, and Job Printing work, at the very lowest cash prices. Legal Blanks of all descriptions always on hand.

One of the largest Book and Stationery establishments in this city is that of Henry C. Lancaster at 829 Seventh Street N. W. Here will be found a full line of Catholic Publications and goods, at the most reasonable prices, of which he makes a specialty.

St. John's Academy is a Military School, at Alexandria, Virginia, six miles from Washington, under the supervision of Richard L. Carne, A. M. This is an old-established school, and is attended by the brightest youth of Virginia and the adjacent States.

The firm of Dobyns and Kimpton, Dispensing Pharmacists, are located in business on the S. E. corner of Second Street and Pennsylvania Avenue, opposite the proposed site of the New Library Building, on Capitol Hill. Here can always be found a full stock of all goods kept in a first-class Drug Store.

STODDART & CO.,

Solicitors of Claims and Patents,

— FOR —

Prosecution before all the Government Departments, Court of Claims, and Committees in Congress.

503 H Street Northwest, WASHINGTON, D. C.

Refers to thousands of clients in all parts of the United States.
Personal attention given to all claims entrusted to us.
Prompt reply to all correspondence.

Springmann Brothers' Express.

Main Office, ... POST BUILDING.
Stables and Warehouse, S. Capitol and D Sts.

Calls for and delivers baggage to all Railroad Depots and Steamboat Wharves. Removes furniture, general merchandise, and heavy machinery.

We give our personal attention. Orders solicited. Special rates to the profession.

P. O. Box 509. TELEPHONE 374-2.

J. W. BOGGS, JR.,

Carpenter and Stair-Builder,

1107 *C STREET NORTHWEST,*

WASHINGTON, D. C.

LANSBURGH & BROTHER,

Nos. 420, 422, 424, and 426 Seventh Street.

The Largest and most Complete Stock in the Line of Dry Goods in this City.

COAST SURVEY BUILDING.

The Coal and Wood Depot of D. P. Lamason, is located at Nos. 812, 814, and 816 Fifth Street N.W. Mr. Lamason warrants every ton of coal to be clean and to weigh 2240 lbs. Coal for family use is made a specialty. Wood, sawed and split, kept under cover.

Wormley's Hotel, corner Fifteenth and H streets N. W., has long enjoyed the reputation of being "par excellence" the family Hotel of Washington. Elegant in its appointments, unexceptionable in its table, it draws a select and refined patronage.

In the same vicinity, at 725 Fifteenth Street N. W., is Welcker's Restaurant and Hotel which enjoys as high a reputation as any establishment of its kind in this city. So famous has become its delicious table that the accommodations for guests have several times had to be enlarged.

W. C. MURDOCK, *Attorney at Law.* E. F. MURDOCK, *Solicitor of Patents.*

MURDOCK & MURDOCK,

SOLICITORS OF

AMERICAN and FOREIGN PATENTS,

OFFICES, 1337 AND 1339 F ST., N. W.,

WASHINGTON, D. C.

KNIGHT BROS.,

PATENT ATTORNEYS

AND EXPERTS,

609 F STREET, NORTHWEST,

WASHINGTON, D. C.

134 BROADWAY, NEW YORK, N. Y.

Consultation and Book of Instructions FREE!

E. B. J. ELLIS,

SOLICITOR OF PATENTS

AND EXPERT IN PATENT CAUSES,

703 SEVENTH STREET, N. W.

OPPOSITE U. S. PATENT OFFICE.

ELLIS SPEAR,

(Late Commissioner of Patents.)

SOLICITOR OF PATENTS,

AND COUNSELOR IN PATENT CAUSES,

927 F Street, N. W.,

LOCK BOX NO. 1. WASHINGTON, D. C.

Special attention given to Interferences, and Examinations as to the scope and validity of Patents. Applications for Patents prepared and prosecuted in the Patent Office.

PATENT OFFICE.—Interior View.

No firm is more favorably known than Messrs. Munn & Co., of 622 and 624 F street N.W., and 361 Broadway, New York city. They have had forty years experience in Patent causes, Copyrights, Reissuess, &c. They conduct their business with the most improved modern facilities, and are always willing to give advice on the patentability of inventions without charge. The Scientific American (Munn & Co., publishers) is circulated widely throughout the United States and all foreign countries.

GONZAGA COLLEGE,

I AND NORTH CAPITOL STREETS,

CLASSICAL AND COMMERCIAL DEPARTMENTS

SHORT-HAND AND DRAWING.

MODERN LANGUAGES.

E. A. McGurk, *S. J., Pres't.*

NATIONAL STABLES,

307, 309 and 311 6th St. N. W., bet. La. Ave. and C Street.

(NEAR B. & P. DEPOT.)

COUPES, LANDAUS, LANDAULETTES, PHAETONS, BUGGIES, SURRIES, &C.

Teams all first-class, with drivers in livery at all hours, day or night.

Branch Offices: { National Hotel, St. James Hotel, Howard House. }

BOARDING HORSES TAKEN.

J. T. PRICE & SONS,

PROPRIETORS.

Telephone call, 115—3.

AT THE RINK.

NEW YORK AVE., BET. 13th and 14th Sts.

THE WASHINGTON INSTALLMENT HOUSE

IS THE PLACE TO BUY YOUR

FURNITURE, CARPETS, BEDDING, STOVES, &C.

The lowest prices and easiest terms of any house in the country. If you want to save money, and have the largest stock in the city to select from, you will

Go to GROGAN'S.

HOUSES UNDERPINNED. OLD FRONTS CLEANED DOWN.

A. DAVIS, JR.,

BRICKLAYER AND CONTRACTOR.

OFFICE, 31 CORCORAN BUILDING.

RESIDENCE, 510 MASS. AVE., N. W.

ESTIMATES FURNISHED FOR BRICKWORK IN ALL ITS BRANCHES.
JOBBING SOLICITED.

BALTIMORE AND POTOMAC DEPOT.

The popular Hatter and Gent's Furnisher of North Washington is Mr. Henry Kreamer, who is located at 1026 Seventh Street N. W. His well assorted stock, including Trunks, Canes, Umbrellas, &c., are sold at the very lowest prices.

The Shaving and Hair Cutting establishment of C. J. Watson is located on the corner of Seventh and D Streets N. W. There are five Bath rooms attached, and an able corps of assistants on hand to prevent delay on the part of customers.

Washington is probably the most enthusiastic city in the country for the National game. The grounds of its Base Ball Club are situated within sight of the Capitol on the corner of G and North Capitol Streets N. E. The accommodations to witness the game are the best in the country, as there is seating capacity for nearly six thousand spectators. The best League games may be witnessed here during the season.

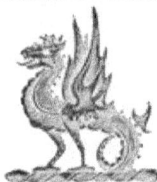

CENTER MARKET—B St. N. W., bet. Seventh and Ninth Sts.

WASHINGTON MARKET CO.

OFFICERS:

MATTHEW G. EMERY,	PRESTON S. SMITH,	SAM'L W. CURRIDEN,
President.	*Supt. and Clerk.*	*Sec'y and Treas.*

Whole length of Market-house on 7th Street, on 9th Street, and on B Street, 740 feet; average width, 82 feet, making .	60,380	sq. ft.
Whole length of Wholesale Store-building, 274 feet, average width, 37 feet, making	10,138	"
Area occupied by Buildings	70,818	"
Area of covered sidewalks	14,000	"
Total space available for Market purposes .	84,818	"
Number of Stalls and Stands	666	
Number of Country Wagons accommodated	300	

MARKET OPEN EVERY WEEK-DAY UNTIL NOON.

SATURDAYS UNTIL 11 P. M.

Charles Yardley, General Commission Merchant, located at 206 Tenth Street N. W., does a large business in consignments of all kinds of Country Produce, Game, Oysters, &c. Persons dealing with him will find him prompt, reliable, and courteous in his treatment of customers. His store is situated conveniently near to Center Market.

HARVEY'S

OLD ESTABLISHED

LADIES' AND GENTLEMEN'S

Oyster Saloon and Restaurant,

1016 PENNSYLVANIA AVE. AND 11TH ST.

U. S. J. DUNBAR, Sculptor.

318 SECOND STREET, S. E.

TEACHER OF MODELING AND DRAWING, PORTRAITS FROM LIFE OR PHOTOGRAPHS IN ANY MATERIAL, SIZE OR STYLE.

SATISFACTION GUARANTEED.

BUSTS AND MEDALLIONS A SPECIALTY.

Academy of the Holy Cross,

—FOR—

YOUNG LADIES AND CHILDREN,

1312 MASSACHUSETTS AVENUE.

—UNDER THE DIRECTION OF—

SISTERS OF THE HOLY CROSS.

HART'S ROACH POWDER.

DEATH TO ALL INSECTS.

For sale by all Druggists and Grocers.

IT CONTAINS NO POISON.

Depot 711 2d Street, N. W.

BEWARE OF IMITATIONS.

ALBAUGH'S OPERA HOUSE.

Those desiring artistically printed Wedding, Visiting, and Society Cards would do well to visit the establishment of Albert Curêt, 934 E Street N. W., who makes a specialty of this kind of work, the excellent character of which his many patrons testify to.

Superfluous Hair is obliterated, leaving no trace, by the Electric needle process, manipulated by Mrs. Dr. Gabriel 614 Twelfth Street N. W. It obviates the use of cosmetics and is specific. Physicians corroborate this statement. A specialty is the treatment of ladies and children by Electricity.

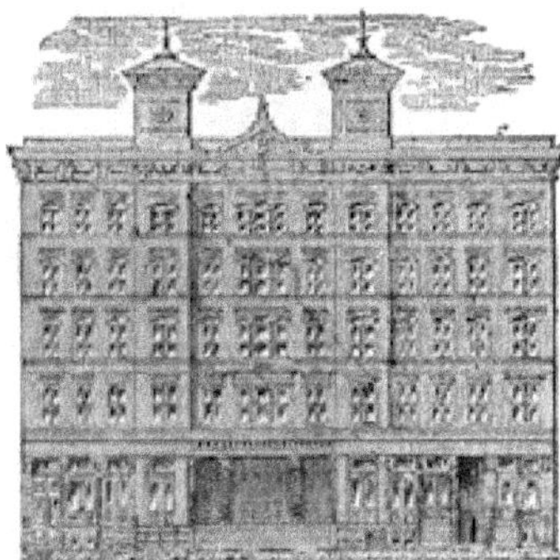

NEW NATIONAL THEATRE.

The only prize medal and diploma for Scientific Engraving at Philadelphia in 1876, was awarded to H. H. Nichols & Co., Designers and Engravers on Wood. The firm is located in Rooms 56 and 57 Le Droit Building, corner Eighth and F streets N. W., opposite the United States Patent Office. They make a specialty of Scientific and Technical Work, Views of Buildings, Inventions, &c. (See page 636 Boyd's Directory.)

Engraving of all kinds of Goblets, Monograms, Original Designs, Initials, and Plain and Ornamental Figuring on Glass is executed by Mr. F. J. Wander, the well-known Engraver on Glass, 907 Ninth street northwest.

The Capital Bicycle Club, the largest in the country, was organized in 1876, and has an active membership of about seventy-five—forty associate, fifteen honorary, and ten non-resident members. They have erected a handsome Club-House, 413 Fifteenth street northwest, near the Treasury building.

CHARLES FLEISCHMANN,

CONFECTIONER AND CATERER,

CAFÈ AND DINING ROOMS,

1410 Pa. Ave., opp. Willard's Hotel, Washington, D. C.

ROOMS EN SUITE.

Orders for Parties, Weddings, Receptions, etc., properly and promptly attended to.

John A. Milburn's Drug Store,

1429 PENNSYLVANIA AVE.,

Near Willard's Hotel, Riggs House and U. S. Treasury.

MILBURN'S POLAR SODA ALWAYS THE BEST.

MILBURN'S PHOSVITÆ.

This great brain and nerve tonic and safeguard against malaria sold in bottles and on draught with Soda Water.

A. LEADINGHAM. T. W. WIDDICOMBE.

CARRIAGES,

COUPES AND HANSOMS,

LEADINGHAM & CO.,

1527 H Street, Northwest,

Branch Office, Willard's Hotel,

WASHINGTON, D. C.

SAMUEL S. SHEDD,

PLUMBING AND HEATING,

Gas Fixtures, Slate Mantels,

LATROBES, GRATES, RANGES, FURNACES.

No. 409 9th St., Northwest, Washington, D. C.

Telephone call, 57-2. Special attention given to Job Work.

WILLARDS HOTEL.

Of Washington hotels, WILLARDS presents, perhaps, the most historic interest. It stands at the head of Pennsylvania avenue. Years ago it was the City Hall. It fell into the hands of the Willard Bros. at the outbreak of the civil war. The name Willards has, in fact, became famous with travellers throughout the Union. With all classes and degrees of American officials, civil and military, it has long been a favorite resort. Politicians have made it their headquarters. It has several times been the starting point of Presidents-elect on their drive to the inauguration. Here, also, many cabinet and foreign ministers have been chosen and military and State papers have been drawn.

The recent improvements of the premises have been liberal and intelligently made. In particular some of the decorations and furnishing of the suites of spacious rooms on the lower floors are very superior.

The excellence of the cuisine has long been appreciated by the community. Fortunately for the public the prices are still reasonable. The present proprietor is Mr. O. G. Staples, a gentleman who has become exceedingly popular with all with whom he has come in contact, by reason of his executive ability, friendliness, and invariable courtesy.

PACIFIC BUILDING.

This handsome building was built in 1885 by Messrs. A. T. Britton and H. J. Gray, prominent attorneys, engaged in practice in Washington under the firm name of Britton & Gray for over twenty years past, whose business has largely been in connection with matters on the Pacific Coast and in the West. The building is of five stories, and contains sixty-five rooms, intended for office purposes. It is furnished with passenger-elevator, steam-heating, deposit-vaults, speaking-tubes, and all modern conveniences. . Its proximity to the Government Departments render it a very desirable location. The firm, which includes, besides the gentlemen named above, Mr. A. B. Browne, occupies a commodious suite of appartments, from No. 51 to 57, inclusive, in the Pacific Building.

PHIL. BEST BREWING CO.'S

MILWAUKEE BEER,

RAEDY & WALSH, AGENTS,

North Capitol and G Streets Northeast.

CHRISTIAN XANDER,

IMPORTER OF AND WHOLESALE DEALER IN

WINES AND LIQUORS,

911 Seventh Stroet N.W.,

Whose business was established in 1866, has gained a trade which extends to all sections of the United States.

The specialty of Mr. Xander's house is his NATIVE WINES, produced from the crops of thirty-three different farms located in Virginia and Maryland. He makes the wine on his own premises. He is an expert distiller, and gives personal attention to tho fermenting and bottling process. The "Clinton" and the "Ives" are known for their flavor, and the "Seedling" and the "Concord" as the cheapest table wines. Mr. Xander is the first dealer in Virginia Native Wines.

J. H. RUSSELL,

Restaurant.

Wines and Liquors Noted for their Purity and Flavor.

1430 NEW YORK AVENUE,

WASHINGTON, D. C.

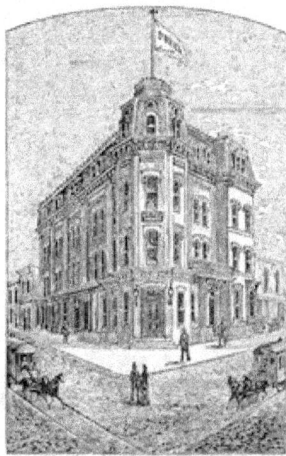

EUROPEAN AND AMERICAN PLAN.

EMMET HOUSE,

Opposite Balt. & Ohio R. R. Depot,

WASHINGTON, D. C.

D. O'BRIEN, . . PROPRIETOR.

WM. MUEHLEISEN,

Importer and Wholesale Dealer in

Fine Wines and Liquors,

AGENT FOR WILHELM QUELLE'S MINERAL WATERS,

— ALSO FOR —

DAVID NICHOLSON'S LIQUID BREAD,

A Pure Malt Extract.

A FULL LINE OF

CALIFORNIA WINES AND BRANDIES.

918 Fifth Street Northwest.

THE CLARENDON

COR. 14TH AND N. Y. AVE., WASHINGTON.

Permanent and transient guests accommodated. The house is centrally located. Cars to all parts of the city pass the door.

It is convenient to all the Departments, Parks, Churches, Theatres, Public Halls, etc. Table, First-Class.

MRS. M. J. COLLEY, PROPRIETOR.

MEMENTOS OF THE WASHINGTON MONUMENT.

Possessing the chips of the Key and Cap Stones of the Washington Monument, the principal stones used in completing that structure, I have manufactured them into handsome jewelry, MOUNTED in SOLID GOLD, such as

CUFF BUTTONS, SCARF PINS,
EMBLEMS, WATCH CHARMS,
EAR-RINGS, LACE PINS, &c.

Ranging in price from $1 to $5.

$1.25. $1.25.

I warrant each article sold by me or my authorized agents to be genuine and from no other stones than those of the Key and Cap Stones of the Washington Monument, the highest structure in the world.

J. KARR,

MANUFACTURING JEWELLER

629 Penna. Ave.,

WASHINGTON, D. C.

SOLID GOLD MOUNTED, $2–$6.50. SOLID GOLD MOUNTED, $2.50–$5.

☞ Orders by mail will receive prompt attention, and articles will be forwarded to any address, postage paid.

EBBITT
HOUSE.

C. C. WILLARD, Proprietor.

The Ebbitt House bears the name of a New York gentleman. In 1865 it was purchased by the present proprietor, C. C. Willard, Esq., who had been previously identified with successful management of the famous Hygiea Hotel, at Fortress Monroe.

Mr. Willard at once began the reconstruction and refurnishing of his new property with characteristic energy. The ground plans were enlarged and the building carried up to seven stories in height. Neither pains nor expense were spared to make the structure perfectly adapted to the purpose for which it was intended. No hotels in Washington (and few in the world) are now better equipped than is the Ebbitt with the essentials for the comfort and safety of guests. A firm spiral stair-case on the outside of the building—the only one of its kind in the city of Washington—renders the establishment practically fire-proof.

Many illustrations might be given to the liberality and executive ability which Mr. Willard bestows, constantly, to maintain the high reputation of his house. His only diversion seems to be to buy and improve property in the neighborhood of the Ebbitt.

The hotel is pleasantly located, on F Street, one block from the United States Treasury. It can accommodate over five hundred guests. The dining-room is attractive and the table generous. While by all classes of the best visitors and residents, this elegant hotel has been long and increasingly patronized, with army and navy people and in diplomatic circles, it has always been especially popular.

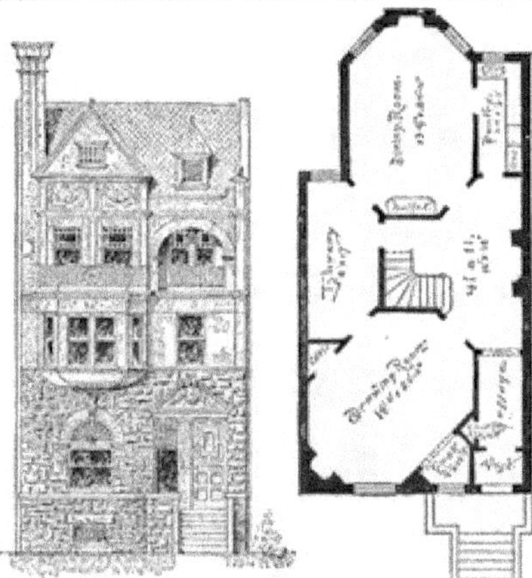

The architecture of Washington has become famous for attractiveness, diversity, and originality of design. It is a common remark of visitors that in no city in the United States is there such a large number of beautiful residences.

Of the architects who have beautified the Capitol with the most artistic and commodious dwellings, none have achieved a more enviable reputation for thorough workmanship and symmetry of design than Mr. Harvey L. Page, lately of the firm of Gray & Page, a sample of whose art—a perfect gem in its way—may be seen above. Mr. Page is located in a very pretty and convenient suite of rooms, at 1515 H Street N. W., where visitors will always be welcome and certain to receive every courtesy, whether intending to engage Mr. Page's professional services, or desiring merely to examine his collection of plans and drawings.

WHITTIER MACHINE CO.

Office and Works, 1176 Tremont St., Boston. Foundry, Cor. Granite and First Sts., South Boston.

MANUFACTURERS OF

Steam, Hydraulic, and Belt Elevators,

BOILERS AND BOILER-PLATE WORK OF ALL KINDS,

Engines, Paper, Rubber and Sugar-Refining Machinery, Hydrants, Water, Steam, and Gas Valves, Ship Steerers, Steam Heating Apparatus, and General Machine Work, Iron and Brass Castings.

NEW YORK OFFICE, 91 LIBERTY STREET, NEW YORK.

CHARLES WHITTIER, President. ABEL C. WHITTIER, Treasurer.

Powell's Patent "STAR" Bath, Basin, Sink, and Tray Plugs WITH RUBBER STOPPERS.

No more denting of copper bath-tubs; no cracking or breaking of earthenware basins, with the use of these RUBBER PLUGS. Plumbers prefer them; architects specify them generally.

Sold by plumbers everywhere, and kept for sale by the dealers in plumbing materials in Washington city. Manufactured by

WM. POWELL & CO.,
[illegible] and [illegible] Front St., Cincinnati, Ohio.

WALPOLE DYE AND CHEMICAL WORKS.

HENRY D. DUPEE,

PROPRIETOR, MANUFACTURER, AND IMPORTER OF

Chemicals, Dyes and Analine Colors,

44 and 46 Oliver Street, Boston.

JOHN C. WELLS,

Elocutionist and Dramatic Reader,

84 West Fayette Street, BALTIMORE, MD.

Private and Class Instruction in Elocution in the most thorough manner. Testimonials from ministers, lawyers, teachers, and public readers. Stammering, Stuttering, and all Hesitancy of Speech remedied by my system of Vocal Culture. Send for circular and terms.

ALSO DRAMATIC INSTRUCTIONS.

The Stenograph,

A SHORTHAND WRITING MACHINE.

Uniform,

Accurate,

Rapid,

Noiseless,

Simple.

This machine for writing Shorthand has been before the public over two years and has met with great favor.

The Stenograph system can be learned in one-third the time required to master even the easiest systems of pencil photography. Stenograph writers can read not only their own notes, but those of other operators as well.

Ladies and gentlemen who have been trained in this system are now holding lucrative positions in this and other cities.

THE TYPE-WRITER.

A Machine that does the work of the Pen.

The writing of this instrument is plain, neat, legible, and business-like.

Professional Men find great relief in the use of the Type-Writer from the drudgery of pen-writing.

The Type-Writer opens up a field of usefulness to young men and women, not dreamed of a few years ago, and furnishes pleasant and profitable employment to thousands of ladies and gentlemen.

For further particulars concerning the Stenograph and Type-Writer call at

Stenograph and Type-Writing Department

— OF THE —

Spencerian Business College,

Corner Ninth and D Sts. Northwest,

WASHINGTON, D. C.

F. K. WARD,

ALDERNEY DAIRIES DEPOT,

The Largest City Dairy in the World,

929-931 D Street Northwest,

WASHINGTON, D. C.

Washington is excellently supplied with milk and butter through several large Alderney Dairies, managed by Mr. Frank K. Ward. The farms are situated in Maryland and Virginia and are conducted in accordance with the most approved principles of scientific farming, to secure richness and purity in the dairy products. Public inspection of the thorough and successful system on which the farms are managed is at all times invited, and will repay any one with a taste for the charms of farm life.

At present more than fifty farms contribute their daily quota of milk, butter, and cream to Mr. Ward's immense establishments; and though the quantity is so great, the quality is never allowed to deteriorate. Mr. Ward has a standing offer of a liberal reward for any persons detecting milk in his cans which is in the slightest degree impure. In these days of inferior cattle, fed with refuse food, this fact is especially worthy of commendation.

F. K. Ward is, undoubtedly, the most enterprising gentlemen in the local Dairy business. His present establishment is the "beau ideal" of his hopes and resolutions. Sketches of him have so frequently been published, that it is not worth while to reprint one here. Without advertisement, F. K. Ward's name will always be among the leading business men of Washington.

M. T. BRIDWELL,

TONIC BEER,

GINGER AND PINEAPPLE ALE,

Soda Water, Lager Beer,

AND

BOTTLING ESTABLISHMENT,

347, 349, AND 351 M ST., BET. 3D AND 4½ STS. S.W.,

WASHINGTON, D. C.

One of the most enterprising business men of this city is Mr. M. T. Bridwell, the well-known Bottler, whose establishment is located at 347–351 M street southwest, near the Arsenal grounds, which now affords a fine park and promenade for the residents of South Washington.

Mr. Bridwell commenced in business at his present location over thirty-five years ago on a small scale, and by industry has extended his premises to cover more than half of the square on which his factory is situated. His trade is not confined alone to the District, but extends into the adjoining States, and is constantly increasing. A number of wagons are employed in the delivery of goods, and employment is given to fifteen or twenty able assistants. Tonic Beer, Soda Waters, Mineral Waters, &c., of various flavors, and all kinds of light summer drinks are manufactured, and in every case warranted to be made from first-class and strictly pure materials.

MANUFACTURER OF FINE BOOTS AND SHOES.

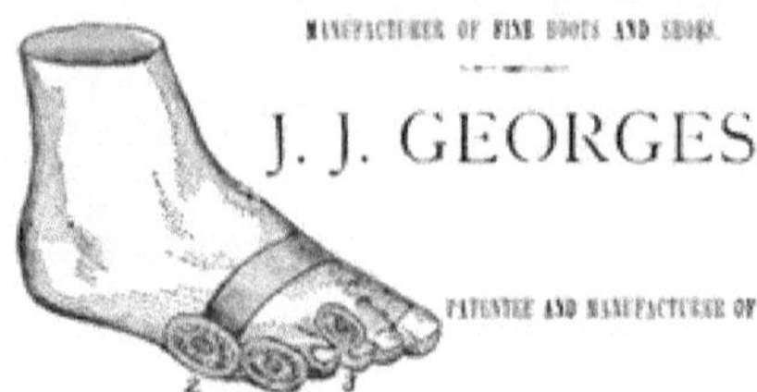

J. J. GEORGES,

PATENTEE AND MANUFACTURER OF

SUPERIOR

CORN AND BUNION SHIELDS,

1208 F Street N. W.,

WASHINGTON.

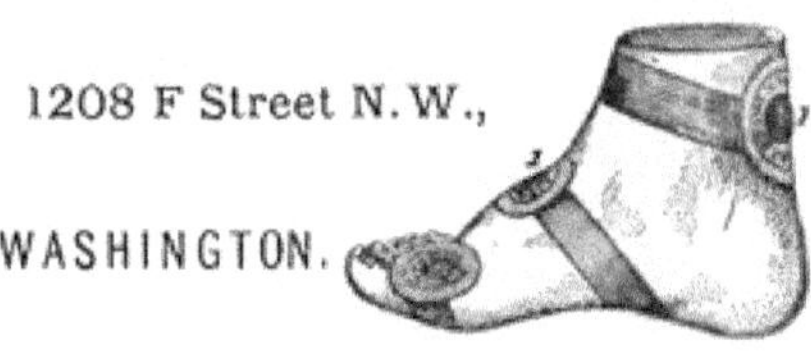

CHIROPODIST.

Orders promptly attended to from hotels and elsewhere.

INSTEP CUSHIONS

A SPECIALTY.

SENT BY MAIL FOR FIFTY CENTS.

JUDD & DETWEILER'S BUILDING.

JUDD & DETWEILER,

NOS. 420-422 ELEVENTH STREET NORTHWEST.

PRINTING OF EVERY DESCRIPTION

In the Highest Style of the Art.

Legal and Scientific Work a Specialty.

PRINTING — BINDING — ELECTROTYPING.

ARLINGTON HOTEL.

The Arlington, corner of Lafayette Square and Vermont Avenue (opposite the White House), is located in the aristocratic part of the City, and is noted for its fine appointments and cuisine. It has been the home of many foreign dignitaries, including Dom Pedro, Emperor of Brazil; Kálu Káua, King of the Sandwich Islands; the Grand Duke Alexis of Russia; Japanese Embassy; Malagassey Embassy, and all the distinguished guests of the Government.

The Hotel is now being elegantly refitted and refurnished, and travelers visiting Washington will be delighted with its comfort.

Messrs. T. Roessle & Son, Proprietors, are also the owners of The Fort William Henry Hotel, Lake George, N. Y., and of the Delavan House, Albany, N. Y.

INDEX.

INDEX.

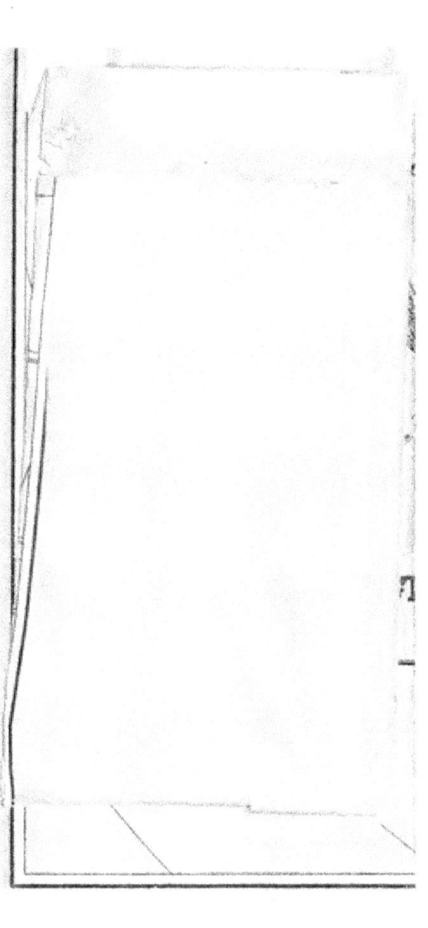

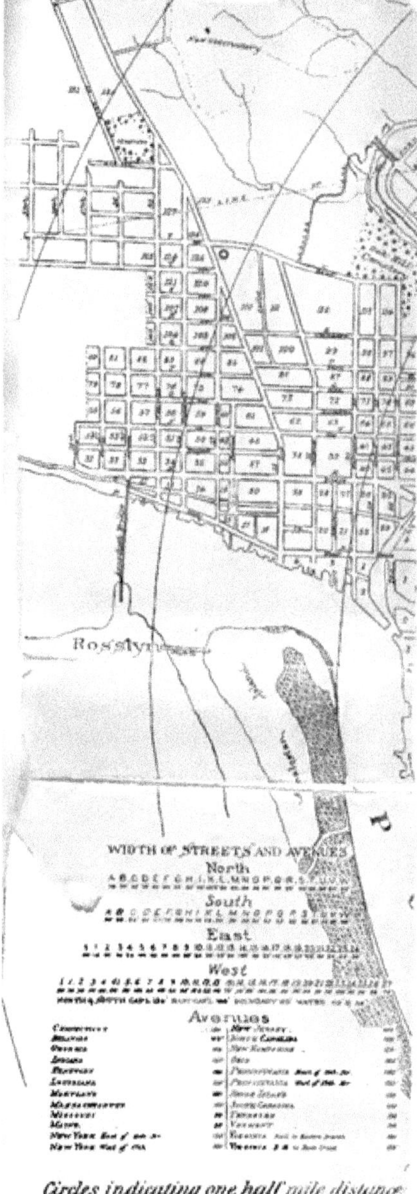

— OF THE —

CITY OF WASHINGT

1891.

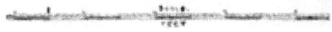

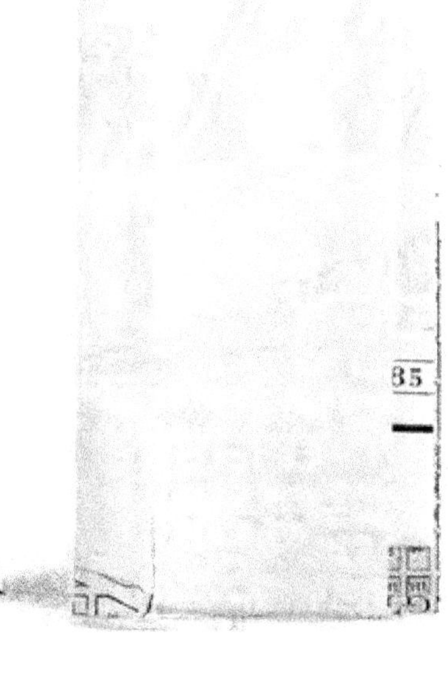

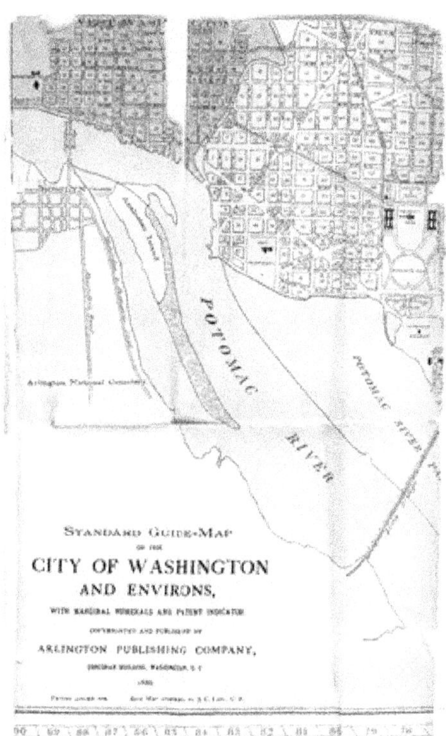
POTOMAC
RIVER
Arlington National Cemetery
STANDARD GUIDE-MAP
CITY OF WASHINGTON
AND ENVIRONS,
ARLINGTON PUBLISHING COMPANY,

www.ingramcontent.com/pod-product-compliance
Lightning Source LLC
Chambersburg PA
CBHW030404270326
41926CB00009B/1254

* 9 7 8 3 3 3 7 1 8 2 4 4 1 *